CULTURE
CATALYST

SEVEN
STRATEGIES
TO BRING
POSITIVE CHANGE
TO YOUR ORGANIZATION

CULTURE
CATALYST

SAMUEL R. CHAND

WHITAKER
HOUSE

Scripture quotations taken from the *Holy Bible, New International Version*®, NIV®, © 1973, 1978, 1984 by the International Bible Society. Used by permission of Zondervan. All rights reserved.

CULTURE CATALYST:
SEVEN STRATEGIES TO BRING POSITIVE CHANGE TO YOUR ORGANIZATION
(Previously published as *Cracking Your Church's Culture:
Seven Keys to Unleashing Vision and Inspiration*)

www.SamChand.com

ISBN: 978-1-64123-078-0
eBook ISBN: 978-1-64123-079-7
Printed in the United States of America
© 2011, 2018 by Dr. Samuel R. Chand

Whitaker House
1030 Hunt Valley Circle
New Kensington, PA 15068
www.whitakerhouse.com

Library of Congress Cataloging-in-Publication Data (Pending)

1 2 3 4 5 6 7 8 9 10 11 𝐋𝐔 25 24 23 22 21 20 19 18

CONTENTS

ACKNOWLEDGMENTS

I acknowledge the thousands of senior leaders who have allowed me to learn from them and their organizations. This book is possible because of their honesty and vulnerability. The contents of this book are a collage of the personal pain and frustration leaders face as they create healthy cultures to fulfill their visions. I also want to thank my friend Pat Springle for working with me to shape the contents of this book.

*To my wife, Brenda; my daughters, Rachel and Deborah;
and my granddaughter, Adeline Joy — they all give up so much to
make my dreams a reality. Because of them, I never lack for constant and consistent encouragement.*

1

CULTURE TRUMPS VISION

Unless commitment is made,
there are only promises and hopes…but no plans.
—*Peter Drucker*

A church in the Midwest grew rapidly, but the growth curve gradually flattened. In recent years, they saw almost no growth at all. In the early days of explosive growth, the senior pastor taught seminars and spoke at national conferences to instruct other pastors in how to grow their churches, but in the past few years, he received very few invitations to speak. When the curve began to flatten, he took his senior staff to hear noted speakers. Surely, he thought, they could learn something new and overcome stagnation. When that didn't fix things, they hired consultants to analyze the situation and prescribe a solution. When this strategy didn't effect the change they wanted, the senior pastor began "cleaning house." He hired and fired so many people that the offices needed revolving doors. Still, the church didn't grow.

Out of frustration, the pastor left the church. He moved his family a few miles away and started another church with about two hundred people who followed him there. Some would call this a church plant; I think it was a glorified church split.

At the original church, a new pastor came into the office full of fresh ideas and a clear vision of where the church could go; that's exactly why he was selected. After a long, grueling first eighteen months with the new pastor on the job, however, the church's growth curve had barely budged. When he called me, he was frustrated and tired. In our first meeting, he told me sadly, "I don't understand. We spent time and money to reenergize the congregation. We took our top staff on a retreat to instill the new vision into them. We hired more staff, and we reformatted our worship experience. We started plenty of new programs. We redesigned our stage set. We created a killer Web site, reconfigured our offices, redecorated to create a fresh ambiance, and designed a new logo for the church. We even wrote a song about how great we are! But none of this has made a bit of difference. We haven't gone backward, and I'm glad of that, but I thought we'd be way ahead of where we are today." He paused for a second and then asked, "What am I missing?"

This senior pastor had done a lot of good things, but he failed to understand the impact of the existing organizational culture on his new, exciting vision for the church. It was like changing the engine on a sports car to make it faster, but it was spinning its wheels in the mud. Or to use a different metaphor, he tried to transplant a heart into a patient whose body rejected the foreign organ. No matter how perfect the new heart was, the patient had no chance at all unless the body accepted it.

Culture—not vision or strategy—is the most powerful factor in any organization. It determines the receptivity of staff and volunteers to new ideas, unleashes or dampens creativity, builds or erodes enthusiasm, and creates a sense of pride or deep discouragement about

> **Culture—not vision or strategy— is the most powerful factor in any organization.**

working or being involved there. Ultimately, the culture of an organization—particularly in churches and nonprofit organizations, but also in any organization—shapes individual morale, teamwork, effectiveness, and outcomes. In an article in the magazine *Executive Leadership*, Dick Clark explains how he took the pharmaceutical firm Merck to a higher level: "The fact is, culture eats strategy for lunch. You can have a good strategy in place, but if you don't have the culture and the enabling systems, the [negative] culture of the organization will defeat the strategy."[1]

To help you uncover the nature of your existing culture and identify the steps of change, this book examines the full range of cultural health, from inspiring to toxic, and describes the seven keys of CULTURE:

1. Control

2. Understanding

3. Leadership

4. Trust

5. Unafraid

6. Responsive

7. Execution

Insight is the first—and crucial—step toward change.

Looking at the Landscape

In the past decade or so, dozens of books and countless articles have been written about the importance of corporate culture, but relatively few churches and nonprofit organizations have taken the arduous (but necessary) steps to assess, correct, and change their culture. First, we need to understand what we mean by the term *organizational culture*. It is the personality of the church or nonprofit. Like all personalities, it's not simple to define and describe. Organization development consultant, speaker, writer, and filmmaker Ellen Wallach observes,

"Organizational culture is like pornography; it is hard to define, but you know it when you see it."

Organizational culture includes tangibles and intangibles. The things we can see are the way people dress and behave, the look of the corporate offices, and the messages of posters on the walls. The intangibles may be harder to grasp, but they give a better read on the organization's true personality. The organization's values (stated and unstated), beliefs, and assumptions; what and how success is celebrated; how problems are addressed; the manifestations of trust and respect at all levels of the organization—these are the intangible elements of culture. Every group in society—family, town, state, nation, company, church, civic group, team, and any other gathering of people—has a culture, sometimes clearly identified but often camouflaged.

Many leaders confuse culture with vision and strategy, but they are very different. Vision and strategy usually focus on products, services, and outcomes, but culture is about the people—the most valuable asset in the organization. The way people are treated, the way they treat their peers, and their response to their leaders is the air people breathe. If that air is clean and healthy, people thrive and the organization succeeds, but to the extent that it is toxic, energy subsides, creativity lags, conflicts multiply, and production declines. I'm not suggesting that churches and nonprofits drop their goals and spend their time holding hands and saying sweet things to each other. That would be a different kind of toxic environment! A strong, vibrant culture stimulates people to be and do their very best and reach the highest goals. Spiritual leaders point the way forward, but they invite meaningful participation from every person at all levels of the organization. Together, they work hard toward their common purpose, and they

> Vision and strategy usually focus on products, services, and outcomes, but culture is about the people—the most valuable asset in the organization.

celebrate each other's accomplishments every step along the way. Trust is the glue that holds the organization together and gives it the strength it needs to excel.

The inputs into the "cultural system" include the stories that surround the staff's experiences; shared goals and responsibilities; respect and care for people; balance between bold leadership and listening; and clear, regular communication. The outcomes include the reputation of the leader, the reputation of the organization, the attractiveness of the church or nonprofit to prospective new staff members, a measure of pride in being a part of the organization, and a positive impact on the entire community.

To see a few snapshots of a church's culture, we might ask these questions:

+ Who are the heroes? What makes them heroes? Who determines who the heroes are?

+ When someone inquires, "Tell me about your church or nonprofit," what stories are told?

+ How much does the average staff member feel he or she has input into the direction and strategy of the church or nonprofit?

+ Who has the ear of the top leaders? How did these people win a hearing with the leaders?

+ What are the meaningful rituals? What message do they convey to those in the organization and those outside it?

+ Who is rewarded, and for what accomplishments?

+ What is the level of loyalty up and down the organizational chart? What factors build loyalty?

+ What is the level of creativity and enthusiasm throughout the organization?

+ When an objective observer spends an hour watching people interact in the offices, what mood does he or she pick up?

+ How are decisions made, deferred, or delayed?

+ Who are the nonpositional power brokers, the people who have authority based on the respect they've earned but who don't have authoritative titles?

+ Where are control problems and power struggles most evident?

+ How is "turf" defined and protected?

The shape of an organization's culture begins at the top level. The leader's integrity, competence, and care for staff members create the environment where people excel...or not. In his book *The Five Dysfunctions of a Team*, Patrick Lencioni observes that trust is the most powerful trait in shaping a positive culture, and trust thrives on honesty. He writes, "When there is an absence of trust, it stems from a leader's unwillingness to be vulnerable with the group," and "leaders who are not genuinely open with one another about their mistakes and weaknesses make it impossible to build a foundation of trust."[2]

I believe that the role of senior pastor is the most glorious and at the same time most difficult in the world. These leaders have the incredible privilege of representing the King of kings, imparting grace and life to people, and creating environments in which God's Spirit changes the eternal destiny—and the present relationships and direction—of men and women, boys and girls in the community. There is no higher calling. Yet senior pastors shoulder enormous burdens. They have to be "on" every time they speak, whether it's to the entire congregation or to an individual. They feel the pressure of finances, deadlines, new visions and missed opportunities, the mistakes and sins of their staff, and their own flaws. But even as they face those troubles, they are expected to be the source of hope, peace, and wisdom for every person in their world. Like the Apostle Paul, senior pastors report either metaphorically or actually, "*I have labored and toiled and have often gone without sleep; I have known hunger and thirst and have often gone without food; I have been cold and naked. Besides everything else, I face daily the pressure of my concern for all the churches. Who is weak, and I do not feel weak? Who is led into sin, and I do not inwardly burn?*" (2 Corinthians 11:27–29). Senior pastors are in a unique position to shape the culture of their teams and their churches, but they can't do it alone. They need the support, wisdom, and commitment of every person on the team.

Let me give a couple of examples of the impact of organizational culture. A senior pastor who understands the importance of creating an inspirational culture has a church with five sites and about a dozen daughter churches. Throughout the organization—from the first interview of a prospective employee to large staff meetings and every team's interaction—staff members remind each other that they come to work each day to make a difference in people's lives. It's not just a job, and they aren't just killing time each day. The pastoral staff has an open-door policy, and they welcome creative suggestions from every staff member. Treating each person in the community and each other with the utmost respect is a high value. The senior pastor regularly carves out time to roll up his sleeves and work alongside the most humble employee at the church.

In an atmosphere of mutual encouragement, top leaders at the mother church, the sites, and the daughter churches are devoted to each other's success, so power struggles are minimized. The senior pastor goes to great lengths to celebrate accomplishments, rewarding not only the vigorous effort to pull off all the work of ministry at the church but also the selfless service to the community. As you can imagine, staff loyalty is through the roof! Staff members express tremendous pride in being a part of such a caring, supportive organization that values them even more than their production.

The senior pastor explained his philosophy of leadership: "I make it a priority to say or do something each day to speak to people's hearts and affirm their commitment to serve God. They work hard, and I want to bring them joy and relieve some stress in their lives. With this as a priority, I find innumerable opportunities to accomplish this every single day. I think about the lives of our staff members and volunteers beyond the walls of our church. They have interests, homes, and families. How they are treated here has an impact on every relationship and every activity in their lives. They need to know I care—and that my expressions of love aren't just words; they're real." The staff at this church come to work each day excited about working as a team to solve problems and make a difference in people's lives. It all starts with the senior pastor's commitment to people and excellence.

The powerful, positive culture of this church is exactly what this book is about—but there are other examples, ones that aren't as inspiring. A friend of mine told me about his experience working at a large church. The senior pastor wore two faces. In public, he appeared to be the paragon of Christian virtue, referring often to Christ, brotherly love, and the Spirit's work in people's lives. In the halls of the church offices, however, he was a tyrant. Those around him observed that power and pride motivated him and shaped his relationships. Once when the pastor faced stiff opposition to a building campaign, my friend heard him snarl, "I don't care if people respect me. I just want them to fear me!" Machiavelli would be proud. Around the office, any semblance of Christian love was blown away by his ridicule of those who made a mistake, and rage at those who offered a suggestion that was different from his intentions. But nobody knew which suggestions would be accepted and which would be blasted. Everyone stayed on edge, fearful of offering an opinion about even the most trivial issue, and waiting for the ax to fall if the pastor disapproved.

The staff enjoyed working with their own teams in their areas of ministry, but they grew to despise the pastor and the circle of yes-men around him. The church lavishly celebrated when the denomination and other organizations gave the pastor accolades, but the staff rarely received even a pat on the back. "Your bonus," the fiercely loyal executive pastor told a competent but beleaguered staff member, "is continued employment. Don't ask for more." The executive pastor smiled as if he were joking, but the staff member knew he was serious.

In this culture, loyalty wasn't earned; it was demanded. When staff members or lay leaders left the church for any reason, they were severely criticized with vicious name-calling. Gradually, most of the competent and emotionally healthy people left the church, leaving behind only those who were afraid to suffer abuse for leaving, or even for considering leaving the church. One of the most alarming facets of this story is that the pastor was commended for several years by his denomination for his "integrity and exemplary leadership." I guess he wrote his own press releases, and enough people believed him. During those years, though, few people bothered to notice the pained expressions on the faces of his staff. Eventually, the diminishing quality of the staff took its toll. The church's numbers stagnated and then declined. Even today, the pastor blames others for every problem he and the church faced. He still doesn't get it.

A healthy culture inspires and stimulates all staff members—whether they're in the boardroom or the mailroom—to give their best because they are convinced their ideas will be valued. In a creative, supportive environment, people are less threatened by their own mistakes and by others' failures. Problems are viewed through a different lens: they become opportunities for growth, not causes for condemnation. Certainly, there has to be a balance between meeting immediate

> In a creative, supportive environment, people are less threatened by their own mistakes and by others' failures.

organizational goals and patient listening, but the vast majority of staff members are thrilled when anyone, especially the top exec, cares enough to listen at all. Employees who feel valued work harder, are more productive, and add value to the organization's purpose. A healthy culture works for everybody.

Key Principles

As we begin our examination of organizational culture, I want to communicate some important principles.

Culture Is the Most Powerful Factor in Any Organization

I travel quite a bit, and I've become a student of hotels around the world. In some cases, I've noticed a significant difference between hotels, even when the rooms actually cost about the same. The difference is in the quality of service. I've stayed in some very nice hotels where it seemed that my coming was a nuisance to the staff. No one opened the door for me or offered to lug my suitcase and boxes into the lobby. From the expression of the person behind the counter, I'm quite sure he would rather have been getting a root canal than checking me in. Sometimes, when I needed some assistance, no one came for a long time, and when they came, they weren't authorized to do what I needed them to do. So I waited even longer. Now don't get me wrong. I had a nice room with clean sheets and fluffy pillows, and I slept very well.

But I've also enjoyed very different experiences at some hotels. Not long ago, I stayed at a Ritz Carlton. When the car dropped me off, a man opened my door and greeted me by saying, "Welcome to the Ritz Carlton, Dr. Chand." I wondered, *Did I leave a nametag on?* No, but somehow he knew I was coming and went out of his way to greet me. The woman at the desk also knew my name (How did they do that?), and she gave me a key without hesitation. Instantly, another man came to help me with my luggage and escort me to my room. He was as kind and attentive as a favorite uncle. My stay was exceptionally pleasant, but a couple of days into it, I lost the key card to my room. As I stood in front of the door, I noticed a cleaning lady down the hall. I asked if she could help me. She instantly let me in and then called for the desk to send up a replacement key. In other hotels, the cleaning people may not be authorized to help in this way, so they have to call for someone else to take care of it. At the Ritz Carlton, though, every staff member has authority to do whatever it takes to care for a guest.

The slogan for the Ritz Carlton Hotels is "Ladies and gentlemen serving ladies and gentlemen." Can you see how this simple but profound statement reflects their inherent corporate culture? By treating each employee with dignity, the company fills his or her need for significance, and warmhearted service flows out of each one like a flood.

I can imagine that the other hotel chains had some kind of written statement to inform employees that they need to serve their guests, but its statement didn't create a culture of service like the one at the Ritz. In fact, it didn't seem to make even a dent. Vision statements, strategies, and goals are very good tools, but they can't compare in importance to the culture. The culture of an organization is the platform for building a strong church or nonprofit. It is the fertile soil for growing creativity and passion for excellence, and the rocket fuel for reaching new heights in excellence and accomplishments.

Culture Is Usually Unnoticed, Unspoken, and Unexamined

How often do we think about the air we breathe? It's so pervasive that we don't even give it a thought. It's absolutely essential for life, but only a few climatologists spend time analyzing it. Organizational culture is like the air; it's all around us, shaping every moment of every day, but we seldom notice it at all.

Sometimes, stepping into a very different culture gives us new insight about our own. When I came to America from India, I came face-to-face with a foreign, distinctly different culture. I had lived my whole life with the spoken and unspoken expectations of Indian life, and the moment I got off the plane in the United States, I knew I was a foreigner in a strange land. For years (and even still today), I've had to be a student of the American culture to know how to relate to people most positively. Sometimes a misunderstanding has led to some good laughs, but it has occasionally created heartache. My experiences in learning to live in a new country have made me aware of the importance of grasping the transforming power of culture.

Most leaders of churches and nonprofit organizations focus almost all their energies on the tangibles of growth and donations.

> Toxic culture is like carbon monoxide: you don't see or smell it, but you wake up dead!

Their means to fulfill their goals are a clear, compelling vision and a workable strategy. Those are important components, but they only succeed if the underlying culture stimulates creativity, passion, and productivity throughout the organization. Top leaders need to spend at least as much time analyzing their culture as they do crafting their new vision, strategy, and marketing plans.

Toxic culture is like carbon monoxide: you don't see or smell it, but you wake up dead!

Culture Determines How People Respond to Vision and Leadership

For one reason or another, some top leaders have an innate distrust of their staff. Their mode of leadership, then, is to tightly control everything their people do. They may smile while they're squeezing employees, but their people don't feel valued when they experience close scrutiny and micromanagement. On the other end of the continuum, a few leaders take a hands-off approach. They think their role is to push the ball and just let it roll wherever it goes. They don't give their staff members direction or feedback, so their people wander around confused and frustrated. Lack of clarity and pervasive ambiguity cannot become the long-term modus operandi. People are left to determine their own goals for their departments and their lives. And some leaders rule by ambivalence and ambiguity. They use the unknown to provoke anxiety and keep people off balance, and then they wonder why people are tentative, indecisive, and nonproductive. In these toxic cultures, people resent leaders instead of respecting them, their level of motivation wanes, they complain a lot to anyone who will listen (and some who don't want to), and they aren't very productive.

> The intangibles of respect and trust transform a church culture into a beehive of thinking, creating, and working together to accomplish grand goals.

The intangibles of respect and trust transform a church culture into a beehive of thinking, creating, and working together to accomplish grand goals. When staff members feel valued, they far more readily embrace a leader's vision. Even if they disagree or don't understand, they are more willing to give the benefit of the doubt and pitch in.

The two examples earlier in the chapter typify the impact of culture on employees' response to vision and leadership. The staff at one church dreaded coming to work each day. They knew that if they were lucky, they'd avoid getting hammered. That's not much of a sense of purpose! In the other church, however, staff members felt tremendously valued— as people, not just as production units—and they were free to offer their opinions about every vision and strategy that came down from the leadership team. In this church, virtually every person loved coming to work each day. Many of them said something like "This environment is the best I could imagine. It's like a family to me. I love working here." And these people worked like crazy because they were convinced that what they did each day really mattered in the lives of people in the community and their fellow staff members, and in their own lives as well.

Whenever I uncover the culture of an organization, I instinctively ask two questions: Would I want someone in my family to work here? and Would I want to work here?

Culture Most Often Surfaces and Is Addressed in Negative Experiences

All of us would like to believe that we are incredibly perceptive and responsive, but the truth is that most of us stay stuck in the same ruts in our lives until something shakes us out of them. These pervasive patterns of behavior are too big for quick fixes. They force us to take a long, hard look at our organizations and ourselves. Only with deep reflection, accurate information, and courage can we take the necessary steps of change.

Make no mistake: most competent leaders rose to their positions because they are supremely confident in their abilities. They're convinced they know how to run the organization, and they've fixed enough problems to fill volumes of books. That's who they are and what they do. But sooner or later, they may run into difficulties that defy their attempts to fix them. Power struggles consume their top levels of leadership, complaints from staff members and church members sour the air each day, and their new vision for growth isn't getting any traction at all among volunteers and the people in the pews. The leaders try this or that, read this book and call that consultant, but nothing seems to work. When the difficulty revolves around people, it's probably a culture problem that won't be solved by any vision or strategy. The only solution is to change the culture.

> Culture problems, by their nature, are never solved quickly.

One of the most important lessons in life is to embrace difficulties and learn from them instead of just trying to get them fixed as soon as possible. Culture problems, by their nature, are never solved quickly. They require a clear understanding of the problem, a commitment to systemic change, and patience and persistence to see change take root.

Almost always, the need to change the culture takes us by surprise. When I came to America in August of 1973 to attend a Bible college, I went to church the first Sunday after I arrived. I listened to the pastor's sermon, and after the service, I passed by him in the lobby of the church. He shook my hand, we talked for a few minutes, and then he graciously said, "If there's anything I can do for you, please let me know."

I responded, "Oh, hell, I'm fine, but thank you very much."

His face turned red, and I quickly realized that I had made my first serious intercultural faux pas. The people behind me moved me along, and one of them whispered to me, "Don't say that word . . . especially in church!"

"What word?" I answered.

He looked pained at my gross ignorance. He winced, " 'Hell.' We don't say 'hell' here."

In India, we said "Oh, hell" the way Americans say, "My goodness." It's not offensive in the least. But in America, I had committed an almost unpardonable crime—in the lobby of a church while talking to a minister! The reactions of the pastor and the man in line behind me told me that I needed to learn something about the culture—and fast!

Far too often, we try to minimize difficulties and act as if they didn't matter, we excuse ourselves and say it's not our fault, or we point the accusatory finger at others. None of these responses leads to wisdom and change. A far more healthy and productive reaction is to stop, notice what happened, and ask, "Is there something more than meets the eye going on here?" That's how we uncover a flawed culture so that we can address it.

Culture Is Hard to Change, but Change Results in Multiplied Benefits

I don't want to minimize the mountain I'm asking leaders to climb. It's a steep and difficult journey, but those who have successfully negotiated it have never regretted a moment on the path. When they see staff members with a compelling sense of purpose, when they hear exciting stories that become part of the organization's history, when they see tears in people's eyes because they believe so much in what they're doing, and when they see them respond with joy and enthusiasm to make a good strategy even better, they know it's been worth it.

How do you know an organization's culture has changed? In his book *The Crazy-Making Workplace*, Christian psychologist Dr. Archibald Hart recounts a conversation with the CEO of a large company. He quotes him: "If you want to know what is really going on in most companies, you talk to the guy who sweeps the floors. Nine times out of

> Talk to people far removed from the seat of power; ask them honest questions about what they see, think, and feel about the organization.

ten, he knows more than the president. So I make a point of knowing what my floor sweepers know—even if it means sweeping the floors with them."[3] If you're a senior pastor, value the input of men and women who love you enough to tell you the truth. Talk to people far removed from the seat of power; ask them honest questions about what they see, think, and feel about the organization. Ask them how people are valued, what motivates them, and what is celebrated. And listen. You'll find out everything you want to know—and maybe more.

So, have you been investing your time and energies into crafting and articulating your organization's vision, only to find that people aren't as receptive as you hoped? When there's a disconnect between a leader's vision and the receptivity of the staff, the problem isn't with the vision; it's the culture. Most leaders don't invest much in their church's culture simply because they assume it's "just fine." I believe, though, that great leaders devote as many resources to building and shaping their organization's culture as they invest in vision and strategy. In fact, vision and strategy simply can't succeed without a positive, healthy culture.

This Book Is for You If...

I've written this book primarily for the top leadership teams in churches and nonprofits, but the principles also apply in the corporate world. The concepts apply to megachurches and small congregations, in every denomination and in independent churches. They work for large, multinational nonprofit organizations as well as mom-and-pop agencies in every sector of service. They apply to parachurch organizations, universities, charter schools, and hospitals.

The commitment to value people all along the organizational hierarchy must be implemented from the top down. The senior pastor and the executive team must lead this effort. When the top leadership team makes a commitment to change the culture, they can use this book to communicate the values and processes to their ministry leaders and other staff members so they are all on board.

As I've talked about these principles to leaders around the world, some have asked if ministry or department heads can implement the changes in this book even if their supervisors don't ever change. Yes, they can courageously take steps to change the culture in their worlds, but they'll always be fighting against the negative pressures from the executive suite. I've known many church ministry leaders and depart-ment heads who "protected" their people from the abuses of their bosses, but they often paid a high price. In most cases, they were glad to do that because they really cared for their people, but eventually, many of these dear, brave men and women were forced out, or they left simply because they couldn't take it anymore.

My Promise to You

If you'll read and reflect honestly on the principles in this book, I believe that you'll have a new appreciation for the impact of your organi-zational culture on every aspect of life. These insights will enable you to make a strong connection between culture and vision so that you always communicate vision *in light of* your culture. A positive culture will act as an accelerant for your vision. With a new appreciation for your cul-ture, you'll empower your staff members to do their very best—and love doing it. You will create the context for vision to grow. When your people feel valued, their enthu-siasm will electrify your church! To make all this happen, this book outlines a process to imple-ment the changes necessary for you, your top leadership team, and all the rest of your leaders.

> A positive culture will act as an accelerant for your vision.

The principles and practices in this book are designed to equip you to be the leader you've always wanted to be. There's no magic formula—quite the contrary. Changing your organization's culture will be one of the most challenging processes you've ever implemented, but I guaran-tee you, you'll be glad you did.

In *Why America Doesn't Work*, Chuck Colson and Jack Eckerd observe, "It would be unrealistic to suggest that managers become per-sonally involved in the lives of each worker. But a sense of intimacy and mutual trust can be instilled in the workplace when managers show gen-uine concern for individual employees."[4] A healthy culture begins at the top, but it eventually releases the creativity and energy of everyone in the organization.

The nature of the topic doesn't lend itself to a quick read and then never being looked at again. Changing the culture of an organization is hard, rewarding work. I've added some reflection questions at the end of each chapter for you and your team to consider, but I'm sure you'll go far beyond these discussions if you're really serious about implementing lasting change. One of the most helpful elements in this book (available on the Web site www.samchandculturesurvey.com; see Appendix 1) is a free diagnostic tool to help you conduct a detailed assessment of your organization's culture. I'm sure you'll find it enlightening.

Think About It . . .

1. Do you agree or disagree with the premise of this chapter that culture trumps vision? Explain your answer.

2. Describe the most inspiring organizational culture you have experienced as a staff member or ministry leader. How did the senior leaders treat people? How did they impart vision and strategy? How did people respond?

3. Why did you pick up this book? What do you hope to get out of reading this book and implementing the steps of change?

2

CULTURE KILLERS

Few things help an individual more than to place responsibility upon him, and to let him know that you trust him.
—*Booker T. Washington*

On a few occasions when I walk into the offices of an organization where I've been asked to consult with the leadership team, I sense immediately that something's wrong. At that moment, it's too early to put my finger on the problem, but after meeting just a few people, I can sense a pervasive anxiety or confusion. If just one person is uncomfortable, I conclude that he or she is having a bad day. If, however, I pick up negative vibes from several people, I wonder if the culture has a systemic problem. The question I always ask myself when I sense a troubled culture is, *Why hasn't someone done something about it already? Don't they see it, too?* The answer is no. The dysfunction in the culture has become entirely normal. It's the way things have been and the way, people assume, they will always be.

Of course, cultures can change, but only when top leaders have the courage to take an objective appraisal of reality. When they don't recognize culture killers, toxic agents continue to infect every corner of the church or nonprofit organization. The first step, then, is to uncover and face the truth. I have the greatest admiration for senior pastors and other top leaders who have the courage and love to step back, take an honest look at their cultures, and take the necessary steps to change them.

Churches and nonprofits have a wide range of personalities. They may produce very different services, but a few common traits characterize healthy organizations, and a set of opposite traits characterizes those that aren't healthy. For our purposes, I want to plot the range of cultures on a five-point continuum:

**Inspiring ... Accepting ... Stagnant ...
Discouraging ... Toxic**

We'll use the metaphor of a race car to illustrate the differences. Think of a high-performance Indy car, finely tuned and built for speed. The car represents the organization's vision and strategy. The car, though, can go only as fast as the road allows, and the culture is the road. Are you ready? Let's take a ride.

Inspiring Cultures

Indy cars fly along the ground at amazing speeds on smooth, dry racetracks. That's the image of inspiring cultures. The spirit of the organization encourages people to bring their best to work each day, and together, they accomplish amazing things.

Characteristics of Inspiring Cultures

+ The leaders of these organizations give clear direction, but they aren't authoritarian; they value the input of every person. Authority is decentralized.

+ Leaders cultivate an atmosphere of trust and respect.

+ People throughout the organization believe that what they do each day really matters—to themselves, to their teams, to the church or nonprofit, and to their constituents. They come to work each day with a compelling sense of purpose, a sense that they are involved in a cause much bigger than themselves.

+ These organizations have high but realistic expectations. They set high goals, train people, give them the resources they need, stay connected throughout the process, and encourage them to succeed.

+ Creativity is rewarded, and failures are viewed as stepping-stones of growth. In fact, failure is seen as an essential part of the process of innovation, not a fatal flaw.

+ There are few if any turf battles, so communication flows up and down the organizational chart and between departments.

+ Top leaders retrain or replace ministry leaders who can't provide a positive work environment for their teams.

+ There is a powerful synergy between relationships and organizational goals.

+ The organization invests significantly and systematically in creating and building a healthy culture.

+ Leaders regularly celebrate success throughout the organization, and they even celebrate those who leave and find success elsewhere.

+ These organizations are a magnet for job applicants. They have their pick of the best and brightest.

Case Study: A Blood Bank with Thirty-Two Branches Around the City

The first thing I noticed when I walked into the corporate offices of this blood bank was how happy the employees seemed to be. Soon I found out why. Jim and his partners had chartered the nonprofit in 1983 in conjunction with a major hospital in the city. From the beginning, they lived by the firm commitment "to serve the community differently."

Jim told me, "I'd worked in several different nonprofit organizations in my career—some really good ones, some not so good—and when we began this organization, I had a very good idea of what I wanted it to become." Before he hired the first employee or opened the doors on the first day, Jim wrote out three lists of commitments he and his staff would make to themselves, their teams, and the people who would give a little of themselves to save others' lives. "These are the benchmarks of our attitudes, our relationships, and our commitment to excellence in everything we do," he explained. He had these three documents made into posters, and put them in every blood bank office and mobile station for everyone to see. "No secrets," he told me, "and no excuses."

At weekly staff meetings in their offices around the city, the branch managers begin by having someone read these three documents to be sure they remain the guiding lights for everything they do in the meeting and during the week. Then, before they get into information, strategies, and problem solving, they spend time sharing stories of how their work has touched people's lives. "For example," Jim related, "last week one of our assistant managers reported how a hospital's blood supply had been dangerously low, and our delivery came at the exact moment when victims of a car accident desperately needed units of blood. With a tear in his eye, he thanked his team for making that crucial, lifesaving moment a reality. Those stories take some time in our meetings, but I think they're the most important things we talk about each week. They light a fire under us!"

Jim learned a lot from his previous experiences in other nonprofits, and he created an inspiring culture for people who work in branches throughout the city. After he told me a few more stories and introduced me to his immediate staff, he looked at me and sighed, "Man, I love these folks"—and they know it.

Accepting Cultures

The road for some churches and nonprofit organizations is fairly smooth, but a little bumpy with a few potholes here and there. On this track, the Indy car has to slow down a bit to be sure to miss the holes and navigate the rough spots. Still, the race car makes great progress. Accepting cultures are very good places to work, for staff, volunteers, and people in the community.

Characteristics of Accepting Cultures

+ The overall atmosphere is very positive, but there are a few topics that are taboo, or there are a few incompetent leaders who remain in the job too long. These unresolved issues and problematic leaders are the bumps and potholes that create tension. In many cases, the difficulties remain isolated in the departments where those poor managers lead. For the people on these teams, the environment may be quite negative, while the rest of the organization thrives.

+ Generally, most people in the organization are supportive of each other's roles and goals. Communication is a strength, and people don't feel the need to defend their turf.

+ Some difficult decisions are avoided instead of addressed expeditiously. For instance, leaving a poor ministry leader in place too long erodes the trust and drive of those who serve in that office.

+ Most people who work in these churches and nonprofits think they are the best ones they've ever experienced. They love the blend of clear goals and strong relationships, and they are highly motivated to do their best.

+ The senior leaders in these organizations invest in developing people and the culture. If they were more assertive about taking care of problems in the culture, they could be even more successful.

+ These organizations enjoy a strong reputation, so they attract a lot of applicants. However, the new hires who are placed under incompetent ministry leaders are deeply disappointed.

Case Study: A Large Church in the South

Every Sunday, almost five thousand people worship at this church in the suburbs of a major metropolitan area. A gifted leader orchestrates the music, and people love to hear the pastor's teaching. When I met with the staff, most of them had glowing things to say about the pastor and the executive leaders. I got a little more insight, though, from talking to a department director. After we talked for a while, I commented on the overwhelmingly positive atmosphere in the church and among team members. "Yeah," he began cautiously, "it's a little *too* positive if you ask me." I asked him to explain, and he said, "Don't get me wrong. I'm all about trusting God and being hopeful, but life isn't always consistently positive. I just wish we were a little more honest about the reality of pain and problems." I asked a few more questions, and he explained, "Oh, we talk openly about other people's problems, but not about our own. Or if we do, we talk about them only after they're resolved."

I asked about the mood of the staff, but he didn't really answer my question. Instead, he remarked, "I think staff members would have to commit a rape and murder to be fired from this church. To my knowledge, there's never been anybody fired, and I don't think there ever will be."

I assumed he was implying that the top leaders were somewhat incompetent in handling staff inefficiencies. "Are you unhappy here?" I asked.

His eyes lit up, "Oh no, Dr. Chand. I love it here. You should have seen the place I came from. It was a nightmare! There are some things here I don't like, but compared to where I've been, this is like heaven!"

Stagnant Cultures

Many organizations begin with a clear vision and great teamwork, but find that sooner or later, their culture loses energy and stagnates. The vision may still be as clear as it has ever been, but the atmosphere is like a humid summer day in Houston—so oppressive it makes you wilt!

In these organizations, the Indy car finds itself on a dirt road full of ruts and holes, a road more suited to a pickup than a race car. To make much progress at all, the car moves slowly to avoid damage. At the end of each day, the driver is worn out but hasn't gone very far.

Characteristics of Stagnant Cultures

- The leadership team sees staff members as production units, not people. The staff members are valuable when—and only when—they produce. All praise is based on performance, very little if any on character.

- Staff members tolerate their leaders, but they don't trust or respect them. They still do their work, but only

- the most ambitious invest themselves in the success of the organization.

- The only heroes are the top executives, and the employees suspect that these top leaders are making a bundle, or at least receiving lots of accolades, at their expense. They resent it, too.

- Without trust, respect, and loyalty, people feel compelled to defend their turf, hang on to power, and limit communication. In this atmosphere, relatively small problems quickly escalate.

- Complaining becomes the staff members' pastime. Things aren't quite bad enough to prompt open rebellion, but a few disgruntled people are thinking about it!

- The leadership team isn't happy with the lack of enthusiasm and declining productivity, so they treat staff as if they were wayward teenagers. They try anything to control them: anger, pleading, threats, rewards, ignoring them, micromanaging them...but nothing works.

- With only a few exceptions, people become clock-watchers and check-cashers, caring little for the leader's vision. The whole organization lives in a status quo of lethargy.

+ To correct the problem, the leaders may send people to seminars or hire consultants, but the top people aren't willing to take responsibility and make significant changes. It's always somebody else's fault.

+ These organizations usually attract people with low expectations and low motivation, but they may attract a few who believe their personal mission is to bring life to the organization. These individuals usually give up after a few months.

Case Study: A Long-Established Church in the Midwest

When I met Sarah, she had been at the church as pastor of singles for about a year. She expressed exasperation with the lethargy and red tape at the church. "I know church work is difficult, and we need to be flexible," she related, "but a little planning by our leadership team would go a long way. I'm trying to make a difference in people's lives, but all I get from them is confusion and delays. The senior leaders say all the right things, but there's very little follow-through. Strange, isn't it?"

I asked if she had communicated her concerns to the people on the leadership team, and she bristled, "About a million times. Too many times, I guess, because now they're branding me as the problem. I used to love this work, but now I think I'm just going through the motions each day. We do some good work for the men and women in our ministry, but it's such a strain to work with the leadership team. I'm on the team, but I feel like I'm on the outside looking in."

I asked, "Sarah, how does your supervisor explain the situation as you talk to him about your vision and your need for support?"

She answered, "He says, 'Sarah, this church has been here for 150 years, and it'll be here long after you and I are gone. This is the way we've always done things, and it's worked pretty well. I think we should just keep doing the same things.'"

I met with several of her staff and key volunteers, and they all were very complimentary of Sarah's leadership. Some of them seemed hesitant to say much of anything to me, probably out of fear that I might talk to the senior pastor, but one of Sarah's administrative assistants volunteered, "Dr. Chand, I know the strain Sarah is under. She's the best thing that ever happened to this church, and she's the best thing that ever happened to me. She protects us the best she can, but she gets pretty discouraged. And let me tell you, if she leaves, I'm leaving, too."

Discouraging Cultures

A few organizations suck the life out of their employees, leaving them hurt, angry, and confused. Every church and nonprofit encounters problems, but good ones make a point of resolving difficulties so that they can rebuild trust and achieve their goals. Discouraging cultures, though, live with the ghosts of countless unresolved problems and unhealed wounds. These organizations may still have clear, bold visions and effective strategies, but their people spend most of their time protecting themselves instead of devoting their energies to the success of the organization. The church's vision and strategy are like an Indy car stuck in the mud. The energy of the engine is wasted in spinning tires.

Characteristics of Discouraging Cultures

+ It's all about the top people: their prestige and their power. They act as though everybody else in the organization exists only to make them more successful, and most of the staff members deeply resent it.

+ People spend as much time trying to survive the power struggles, protecting themselves from more hurt, and analyzing the top people's pathology as they spend doing the work of the ministry. Staff may become fiercely loyal to a supervisor who protects them, but they actively seek to undermine any perceived adversary.

+ As the benchmarks of success decline, the top leaders become more authoritarian and threatening. They demand compliance and loyalty, and they defy anyone who disagrees with them or even offers another opinion. One man who worked in a nationally known church told me, "The ministry director told me that I had to work eighty hours a week or I could leave. I'm a salaried employee, so I don't get overtime. Basically, he was saying, 'We don't care about you at all. We *own* you.' That day, I started looking for another job."

+ The leadership team often tries to remedy the problems, but with the wrong analysis and the wrong solutions. They seldom look in the mirror to find a culprit. Instead, the blame is always put on "incompetent" or "unmotivated" people throughout the organization, but these are the only ones who are willing to stay employed there! Leaders may ask staff members to go to seminars and workshops, and they may even hire consultants from time to time, but they seldom listen to any outside input.

+ When these leaders communicate a new vision, nobody cares. They've heard it before, and they don't trust that anything will be different this time.

+ These organizations attract malcontents, sycophants, and desperate people who can't find a job anywhere else.

Case Study: A Youth Ministry in the Middle Atlantic States

John is the director of twenty youth ministries in three states. About seventy-five staff members and volunteers report to him. He was hired because of his reputation for caring for staff. The previous director had been quite goal oriented, instituting a rigid set of performance expectations and reviews. The nature of people who are attracted to the staff of youth ministries, though, is highly relational. The local leaders chaffed under the former director's leadership, and he bruised a lot of them by insisting on their compliance "no matter what."

When John was hired, they said they wanted him to breathe fresh air into these staff members, but soon he realized that he was suffocating in the smog of the board's resentments and demands. He found himself in the middle of a power play among several powerful, wealthy men on the board. For over a year, he was caught between warring factions on the board; sky-high demands for staff performance (didn't they hire him to change the culture?); and misunderstandings by his local staff, who were upset that he wasn't able to implement change any faster. By the time I saw him, John was experiencing stress-related medical problems. He had come into his role full of confidence that he was a competent leader. "Now," he related with obvious sadness, "I don't know if I can do anything right anymore." He called me because he wanted my advice about dropping out of ministry.

Toxic Cultures

Strangely, some of the most toxic organizations have the most charming leaders. To people on the outside looking in, these senior leaders and nonprofit executives present themselves as gracious, gifted leaders, but those who see them every day are the victims of their fangs and venom! In these cultures, the Indy car is on the road, but the bridge is out! Disaster is waiting for those who stay on board.

Characteristics of Toxic Cultures

+ Leaders create a "closed system," so any advice and creative ideas from the outside are suspect from the start. In his insightful book *Incest in the Organizational Family*, William White observes that these systems breed bad ideas, bad behaviors, and bad values into the organization over and over again. That's why he calls it incest.

+ Individual rights and the dignity of staff members are surrendered to the powerful elite. People are expected to do as they are told—nothing less and nothing else. The organization's leaders believe they "own" every employee. They have exceptionally high expectations of workers, but they offer them little or no autonomy to make decisions.

+ Fear becomes the dominating motivational factor of the organization, and those who choose to stay meekly comply—most of the time. Many, though, are too afraid to leave. They've noticed that when people even think about leaving, they're severely criticized for being "disloyal."

+ Turf battles are the accepted sport of the organization, and open warfare becomes normal. Suspicion and resentment poison lines of communication, so even the simplest directive becomes a weapon.

+ Leaders delegate responsibility but fail to give authority to people to fulfill their roles.

+ Creativity and risk-taking have long vanished, and in fact, these traits threaten the status of the bosses as the only ones who know anything. In this environment, pathology is rewarded and health is punished.

+ Ethical, financial, or sexual lapses may occur, but staff members are expected to turn a blind eye. The leaders may constantly look over their shoulders to see if they've been caught.

+ These organizations run off good people, and they attract only the naïve or truly desperate.

Case Study: A Hospital

I talked with a woman who had been an administrator at a hospital in another city before she moved to her new position. "I had to get out of there," she told me. "It was a disaster." She related that her previous boss was a tyrant. "He was often asked to speak at civic functions around the city and even at churches from time to time, and he gave wonderful talks about our hospital being a place of hope and healing. But no one in the office trusted him. We had to warn any woman who came to work in our department that she might be a target of his sexual advances. Some of them listened; some didn't. One of them got pregnant and had an abortion."

I asked if she had talked to the hospital's human resources department. She laughed, "Oh, I tried several times. They talked to him, and he convinced them that I was blowing it all out of proportion." The damage, however, wasn't limited to the boss's sexual targets. "Everyone in the office suffered," she related. "Never did we feel safe and appreciated. I stayed as long as I could, but when I had the chance to leave, I took it." She explained that he was finally exposed, fired, and charged. "I hope they found a good person to take his place. Just think," she lamented, "all that happened in a place of healing. Very strange."

In my experience, the spectrum of cultures I've described falls along a bell curve. I've found relatively few truly inspiring organizations, but thankfully, I haven't encountered many that are genuinely toxic. Most churches and nonprofits fall in the middle three categories. Looking at the top end of the scale, we shouldn't assume that inspiring and accepting organizations simply don't have problems and that this is why they excel. Quite the contrary. They all experience difficulties, but the leaders of healthy organizations are steadfastly committed to resolving problems, not with a heavy hand to rigidly control people, but by treating everyone with respect. They work hard to continue to build their cultures, taking nothing for granted. An incestuous organization continually breeds bad genes back into the system, but healthy companies invite new ideas and creative input from every imaginable source. A significant element of their stimulating environment is their thirst for growth and development.

Potholes, Mud, Pits, and Collapsed Bridges

The most powerful features of an organizational culture are trust and respect. With them, almost any problem

> The most powerful features of an organizational culture are trust and respect.

can be resolved, or at least people learn valuable lessons from difficult experiences, and in the process even learn to trust each other more. But without trust and respect, even the smallest molehill soon morphs into an Everest. The most common hazards we face are:

Unrealistic demands

Blaming others

Feeling threatened by others' success

Power struggles

Dishonesty

Creating an atmosphere of fear

Using people instead of valuing them

Unclear vision, strategy, goals, and values

A lack of authenticity

Let's look at some of the potholes, mud pits, and collapsed bridges that threaten to slow, stall, or crash our Indy car.

Unrealistic Demands

There's nothing in the world wrong with having high expectations of staff members, so long as there is always a healthy dose of realism in an atmosphere that welcomes give-and-take, creativity, and problem solving at all levels. Let's be honest. Leaders of churches and nonprofits shoulder enormous responsibilities. When times are tough, the easiest thing for them to do is pressure their staff to work harder and longer. These pressure points, though, are watershed moments for organizations. I've seen some leaders go to their staff, explain the difficult situation they're in, and say something like, "I know I'm asking for a lot, but here's what I need you to do. I'm in it with you, and together, we'll get through this." In these cases, the vast majority of staff members respond by rolling up their sleeves and working tirelessly, and the experience builds the bond between them and the leadership team. But too often, I've been called in after the leader damaged people and eroded their trust in him by simply demanding "more bricks with less straw"—a sure recipe for resentful staff!

Leaders may communicate unrealistic expectations in any area: deadlines, workload, skills, training, communication, or productivity.

In dysfunctional cultures, however, any question from an employee is met by an angry response: "I don't care what it takes. Just get it done!"

Blaming Others

One of the most trust-building statements any leader can make is, "I'm sorry. I was wrong." Most of us have no idea how much it means to our staff when we take responsibility for our blunders. Almost nothing builds trust like a leader's accepting responsibility, and almost nothing destroys it as quickly as blaming others for one's mistakes. Some leaders try to wear Teflon, hoping nothing will stick to them when problems occur. They fail to realize that a responsible, heartfelt response to a single failure may do more for their culture than a hundred successes.

> One of the most trust-building statements any leader can make is, "I'm sorry. I was wrong."

Feeling Threatened by Others' Success

Some leaders desperately want to appear supremely confident but actually are terribly insecure. They demand to be the center of attention, the go-to person for the organization, and they feel threatened when anyone else succeeds or receives applause. These leaders may occasionally smile and pat successful people on the back because they know it's expected of them, but perceptive staff can tell that their smile hides a grimace.

Power Struggles

When organizations don't enjoy an atmosphere of trust and respect, they quickly degenerate into a law of the jungle and survival of the fittest mind-set. Fitness, in toxic cultures, is measured not by competence but by cunning. Everyone longs for security and significance, but without trust, the only hope of achieving these goals lies in hiding to avoid trouble or in beating others to the top. In these organizations, people often form

Fitness, in toxic cultures, is measured not by competence but by cunning.

alliances—just as contestants do on the reality show *Survivor*. People secretly plot against each other, forming secret (or not so secret) alliances. Gossip, deception, lies, and sabotage become chess pieces in the game. In the end, everyone loses, even those who thought they won, because those who watched them as well as those who participated lost respect for people playing the game. People engage in these games at every level of corporate life, from the senior pastor's office to the loading dock. Without trust and honest communication, these games are inevitable... and destructive.

Dishonesty

Some leaders may be able to fool some of the people some of the time, but they can't fool all the people all the time. Sooner or later, their dishonesty will come back to bite them. To make themselves look good and others look bad, they may exaggerate just a bit, or they may outright lie to anyone who will listen. People treasure truth, fairness, and justice, so deceptive leaders shatter their reputations, breaking trust with those whom they need most to run a successful organization.

Creating an Atmosphere of Fear

Fear, I believe, is one of the most powerful motivators in the world—and one of the most destructive. The reason so many leaders use it is that it's very effective, and when these leaders see how it controls people's behavior, the effect is almost addictive. Outbursts of anger, cutting criticism, isolation, gossip, and a host of other painful actions may be directed at a single person, but the incident affects everyone who watches, listens, or even hears a rumor about it. Harsh words and deeds don't have to happen every day to destroy a ministry environment. Even occasional outbursts of anger and condemnation stick in the minds and hearts of the staff to create the fear that such outbursts could happen again—and could happen to them!

Angry leaders soon become convinced that fear works very well as a motivational tool, and they close their eyes to the damage they cause. Soon it becomes a normal part of the organization's culture. People learn to dance around it, hide from it, excuse it, and absorb the blame for others' misbehavior. Leaders who use fear to control people, however, need to remember that there are other, better ways to motivate people. Investment banker Charles Schwab commented, "I have yet to find the man, however exalted his station, who did not do better work and put forth greater effort under a spirit of approval than under a spirit of criticism."

Using People Instead of Valuing Them

Do you think people can tell if their leaders value them or are just using them for their own selfish ends? A few unperceptive staff members may not be able to tell, or they may be so happy to have a job that they're willing to put up with it, but most of them inherently resent being seen as things instead of people. They want to be more than cogs in someone's machine, more than a cipher on a spreadsheet of production, and more than a servant to respond to another's wishes. They long to be seen as people of value, and they do their best work when they feel appreciated. Australian entrepreneur John Ilhan observed, "If you treat staff as your equal, they'll roll their sleeves up to get the job done."

Unclear Vision, Strategy, Goals, and Values

People don't thrive in confusion. When a leader charts a clear course, the staff may ask a lot of questions before they get on board, and some may drag their feet for a long time before they embrace the skipper's map, but understanding is an essential element of a healthy work environment. Some leaders don't invite questions when they make their pronouncement of

Unpredictable leaders produce tentative followers.

the future. Maybe they're not too sure about it themselves. And a few leaders believe that a slick presentation should wow people enough that they won't have any questions at all. A clear grasp of the direction of the organization, though, is essential for there to be alignment and teamwork in each area of ministry. Without it, people wander, complain, doubt their leaders, chart their own course, or leave to find better leaders. Unpredictable leaders produce tentative followers.

A Lack of Authenticity

People thrive on genuine appreciation, but they bristle when they sense that affirmations are less than sincere. A staff member of a megachurch told me, "I wish the ministry director wouldn't ever try to compliment me. Every time he does, it seems so contrived, forced, and insincere. I'd much rather hear nothing than that." It's not enough for leaders simply to say the right things; their people have to believe that in the depths of their hearts, the leaders mean them—and they shouldn't say them until and unless their words can be genuine. For some, this presents a problem: they simply can't seem to muster sincere appreciation for others. The difficulty, though, isn't in the leader's personality. I believe God made all of us with the capacity to show genuine thankfulness to Him and to people. The problem is that some leaders resent the fact that they aren't getting as much praise as they're expected to give out. Their emotional tank is empty, and they hate filling up someone else's until theirs is filled.

> People around us can sense when we're being sincere and when we're phony.

People around us can sense when we're being sincere and when we're phony. They despise phoniness, but they thrive on sincere appreciation, even if it's not as frequent or as eloquent as they'd like it to be. A lack of authenticity in appreciation further erodes trust and creates doubt among the troops.

Very few senior leaders of toxic environments read books like this. The last thing they want is an objective appraisal of the dysfunction in their organizations. However, a few find the courage to made drastic changes. And top leaders across the rest of the spectrum long for their churches and nonprofits to be strong, healthy places where people thrive, support each other, and celebrate each other's successes. That, they are convinced, is the key to genuine success for their organizations, their leadership teams, their staff members, and those they serve. They have learned to be wary of the culture killers and address them quickly when their ugly heads arise.

Think About This . . .

1. Think of the organizations where you've worked or, if you've worked only in one for a long time, think of the departments where you've worked. Where would you put each of these on the spectrum of cultural health?

   Inspiring...Accepting...Stagnant...Discouraging...Toxic

2. Pick one of those experiences and jot down the characteristics (positive and negative) from this chapter that describe it.

3. Review the list of potholes, mud, pits, and collapsed bridges in the second part of the chapter. For each one, rate on a scale of 0 (not in the least) to 10 (all day every day) the degree to which your leadership reflects these problems:

   ____ Unrealistic demands

   ____ Blaming others

   ____ Being threatened by others' success

   ____ Power struggles

   ____ Dishonesty

   ____ Creating an atmosphere of fear

   ____ Using people instead of valuing them

____ Unclear vision, strategy, goals, and values

____ Lack of authenticity

4. What does this exercise tell you about yourself? What does this exercise tell you about your organization?

3

SEVEN KEYS OF CULTURE

*To look at something as though we had never seen
it before requires great courage.*
—*Henri Matisse, painter*

Have you ever walked into an office and, after only a few casual, brief conversations with people, sensed something was wrong? Many of us have a sixth sense about the atmosphere and relationships on a team, but it's much easier to take a sniff test in someone else's church, office, store, team, or home than our own. Amazingly, some of us who are incredibly perceptive about other cultures are clueless about the nature of relationships and attitudes around us each day. To be objective, we need to step back from time to time and take a good, long look in the mirror. We might be surprised at what we see.

People have an almost limitless capacity for self-deception. We don't know what we don't know and are therefore unconsciously incompetent. If we were aware of our deficits, we'd ask questions and find solutions, but because we're not aware, we stay stuck in the status quo until something shakes us awake.

> We don't know what we don't know and are therefore unconsciously incompetent.

Quite often, we need some help to see things clearly. We are simply too close to the people and systems in our own environment to be objective. To change the metaphor: you wouldn't ask a fish to tell you how water tastes because it doesn't have objectivity. Only someone from the outside (or perhaps some penetrating questions from an outside source) can help a fish analyze the purity of water—or assist us in taking an accurate read on the health of our culture.

Beyond Excuses

When I talk with leaders and teams about creating a new culture, many of them instantly realize the beauty and power of working together in an inspiring environment, and they commit themselves to do whatever it takes to achieve it. Others, however, find creative excuses for remaining stuck in the past. I've heard people say they can't take steps forward because

"I'm too new to the team. No one would listen to me." "I only have three years left before I retire. It seems like it would take too much out of me to try to change our culture."

"The price is too high. I'm not willing to take those risks."

"I can't do everything. We're starting a building campaign, and I need to devote my energies to that."

"I've been trying to cast a vision for the future, but people just don't get it."

"Every time I try to talk about our culture, people get defensive. I've had it!"

Analyzing a team's culture is a lot like marriage counseling. The way people relate to each other and the way things get done are entrenched patterns that have been in place for years. These patterns frustrate people, but nobody talks about them until someone from the outside addresses the core issues of culture, connection, and communication. When I consult with pastors and teams, I often begin by asking, "Imagine your team is the U.S. Congress. How does a bill get passed here?" Quite often, people roll their eyes or laugh in a passive-aggressive way. They feel uncomfortable because I've asked a question that addresses more than surface issues. I've probed into the heart of their culture. I pause and let them realize that my question wasn't rhetorical, and then they really get nervous! After an awkward moment, one might say, "Well, we talk a lot, but not much gets done." Or someone might assert with a flash of anger, "We all have different ideas about how to do things, but we can't seem to come to a conclusion." Or more telling, a person might grumble, "I'm not sure if my input matters much, about this or anything else."

> Imagine your team is the U.S. Congress. How does a bill get passed here?

To help the team members uncover their needs and desires, I often ask, "If the meeting ended right now and you could make one suggestion to the pastor (or team leader) to improve the church or the team, what would it be? Anything goes. What would you suggest to him?" Recently, when I asked this question in a team, the responses included,

"Better strategic planning."

"Implement what we plan instead of just leaving the plans on a piece of paper."

"Clear communication and coordination." "Empower people to do what they're asked to do." "Simplify the strategy."

"Add strength and value to the present team." "Relax more and enjoy what we do."

"Clear and simple opportunities to engage the vision." "Hold people accountable."

"Plan ahead, and include us in the planning." "Celebrate our achievements."

"Stop changing the goalposts."

Their answers told me volumes about their culture. These suggestions surfaced their perceptions of their current environment. Without saying, "Pastor, I don't feel valued by you, and I'm afraid you're going to replace me with someone else," the person communicated the same idea by suggesting that the pastor "value the present team." Words matter, and they often carry multiple meanings.

People might think that pastors become defensive and resistant when their people give these suggestions, but quite often, I've noticed a spirit of genuine openness. Pastors and team leaders genuinely want to be the best leaders they can be. Many of them spend thousands of dollars each year attending conferences to learn to fulfill their roles more effectively. When the issue of culture is raised, they simply haven't known the right questions to ask to get below the surface to talk about the team's environment. When I ask these questions and pastors hear their staff members' responses, they are often surprised, but they always want to talk more about their perceptions. Then, when we talk about culture, they often report, "I've never heard that before" or "I didn't know that." Leaders and team members need to start with a few questions that help them look in the mirror to see what's really going on. Insight provides choices, and these choices become steps in creating a vibrant culture.

Pastors and business leaders report that it's relatively easy to institute a new program or introduce a new product, but changing the culture is the hardest thing they've ever done. It requires wisdom, courage, and tenacity, but it begins with an understanding of the current condition. A few simple metaphors help them see the importance of addressing the culture of their organizations. I often explain that it doesn't make sense to serve a lovely dinner on a dirty plate, and a doctor can't perform a kidney transplant until the patient is free from infection. A stagnant, discouraging, or toxic culture is like the dirty plate and the infection. Very little progress can be made until the plate is washed and the disease is healed. But once they are, dramatic progress is possible. Leaders (and their team members) instinctively understand these metaphors. As I shared this concept with one pastor, he told me, "Dr. Chand, this is incredibly helpful. For a long time, I thought I needed to charge up my team by finding just the right program. When that didn't work, I tried to be more

> It doesn't make sense to serve a lovely dinner on a dirty plate, and a doctor can't perform a kidney transplant until the patient is free from infection.

passionate about our vision, but the more intense I became, the more passive they got. I've tried all kinds of things. Some worked for a while, and of course, some worked better than others. But now I realize that I've been trying to serve a steak dinner on a dirty plate. No one wanted to receive what I was presenting. We have to clean the plate. Will you help me?"

A Glimpse of the Culture

I want to invite you and your team to look in the mirror to see the nature of your culture. The categories of "healthy" and "unhealthy" aren't very helpful because they aren't specific. To go deeper, we'll examine seven important factors that shape organizational culture, and for each of these, we'll identify particular attitudes and behaviors that point a culture toward either inspiration or toxicity. The seven keys of CULTURE are

1. Control

2. Understanding

3. Leadership

4. Trust

5. Unafraid

6. Responsive

7. Execution

As we examine these, don't focus on yourself. Instead, take the temperature of your whole team. Culture is about relationships, communication, and shared values, not just about an individual's perceptions and behavior.[1]

Control

People function most effectively if they are given control (or authority) with responsibility. If they are held accountable for a task without having the means to accomplish it, they'll fail, and they'll be terribly frustrated.

On the other end of the spectrum, if control is concentrated in one person who insists on making virtually all important decisions, the organization experiences a significant bottleneck. It should be a warning if everyone is expected to consult with one person about everything before moving on. Bottlenecks affect every person on the team, not just the one who is waiting for an answer. Isn't it odd (and thoroughly predictable) that when one lane of traffic is blocked on the interstate, all the lanes slow to a crawl? Teams thrive when there is a free flow of information and ready access to resources.

Contrary to the beliefs of some people, *control* isn't a dirty word. Delegating responsibility and maintaining accountability are essential for any organization to be effective. Strong, effective teams have a "Goldilocks approach" to control: not too much, not too little, but just the right amount of checks and balances. The leader gives clear direction, assigns tasks, delegates authority, provides resources, and then has a reasonable reporting procedure so the person can provide updates, coordinate with others, and stay on track until the task is finished. The right control system for a team is like a conveyor belt of ideas and resources. It manages the flow of work—not to slow it down, but to make it flow smoothly and effectively.

Quite often, the real power broker on a team isn't the person at the head of the table. Good leaders involve everyone in the planning process, but sometimes an angry, sour, or demanding person can dominate a team. A sure sign of problems with control on a team are turf issues. When two or more people believe they have responsibility and authority for a task, they compete

> Turf battles are about personal pride and perceived power.

with each other for resources and, even more, for supremacy over each other. Turf battles really aren't about the tasks people fight over; they are about personal pride and perceived power.

Team members need to see themselves as partners in a grand venture, not competing for control over others, not carving out territory to defend to the death, but using delegated authority for the common good.

Here and in the next sections, I want to ask a few questions to help you analyze each element of your culture.

Take a Look

+ Are lines of authority and responsibility clear on your team? How can you tell?

+ Do people know what is expected of them, or are they confused sometimes?

+ What do turf wars look like on your team? What are they really about?

+ Would you say there is too much control from the top on your team, too little, or just the right amount? Explain your answer.

Understanding

Every person on a team needs to have a clear grasp of the vision, his or her role, the gifts and contributions of the team members, and the way the team functions. Each person should be able to clearly articulate each of these vital aspects of the team's life.

The vision must be both global and specific—too big for anyone to accomplish without the power of God, but with handles on each person's specific role in fulfilling aspects of the overall vision. It breaks my heart when I talk to a staff member who says glumly, "I'm not really sure what I'm doing here."

Healthy, strong teams can point to one another and say things like, "Bill is really good at that," "Crystal understands this system really well," or "Kim has experience in helping people with that issue." Knowing one another and appreciating each person's contributions grease the wheels of progress on a team. How do we know what makes each other tick? By taking time to hear each other's stories. In staff meetings or during an hour over coffee, we can find out more about someone's heart and experiences than we could learn in years of sitting in meetings together. All it takes is a little time and a few caring questions.

Team communications are everybody's responsibility. Certainly the leader's task is to make sure each person clearly grasps the principles and delegated tasks, but good teams normalize the question everyone can ask: "Would you explain that again? I'm not sure I got it." In this way, misunderstanding is never an excuse for not getting the job done. Similarly, before a meeting is over, the leader can ask each person to share priorities, schedule, and coordination needed with other team members. This way, everyone is on the same page.

Understanding, though, isn't just about the *what* of ministry; it's also about the *why*. Again, grasping the underlying concepts is everybody's job. Leaders need to take time to explain how a new program fits into the plan, why it will make a difference in people's lives, and the important role each person will play in making it successful. Team members are encouraged to take initiative to ask questions so they understand these things, even if the leader forgets to explain them.

Take a Look

+ Is the vision for your team both God-sized and specific? Explain your answer.

+ Do people on the team feel understood, valued, and directed to give their best each day?

+ Do most lines of communication on the team flow from the leader, or is there good cross-pollination? What's the result of this flow?

+ How do people on the team respond when someone asks "Why?"?

Leadership

Healthy teams are pipelines of leadership development. They recognize that an organization is only as healthy as the pool of rising leaders, so they actively seek to *discover* those who show leadership potential, *develop* resources to equip and inspire leaders, and carefully

> Healthy teams are pipelines of leadership development.

deploy them in roles that enflame their hearts, challenge them to excel, and propel the organization to new heights.

We need to make a distinction between leadership and management. To develop people to become leaders, we focus on heart and character. Training is important, but it's a management issue, equipping people to perform a particular task. Both are significant, but developing people is far more essential in creating a healthy culture than training people in specific skills. Plenty of toxic and discouraging cultures have highly trained, efficient staff members. They know how to do their jobs very well, but their culture stinks.

Let me highlight the differences between leaders and managers:

Leaders	*Managers*
Conceptualize outcome by working from the FUTURE back to the PRESENT	Conceptualize plans by working from the PAST to the PRESENT
Embrace a MACRO—big picture— perspective	Embrace a MICRO—snapshot— perspective
Favor INNOVATIVE thinking	Favor ROUTINE thinking
Possess REVOLUTIONARY flair	Are PROTECTORS of the status quo
Emphasize the WHAT and WHY	Emphasize the HOW and WHEN
Are INSPIRING and motivating	Are CONTROLLING and directing
Are EXCITED by change	Are THREATENED by change
Move QUICKLY	Move SLOWLY
Identify OPPORTUNITIES	Identify OBSTACLES
Take RISKS	Avoid RISKS
Pursue acquisition of RESOURCES	Are bounded by AVAILABLE resources
Are PEOPLE centered	Are SYSTEM centered
Are IDEA centered	Are PLAN centered
Perceive people's approval as a WANT	Perceive people's approval as a NEED

Summary: Managers get the most out of themselves. Leaders get the most out of others.[2]

Many church teams focus on training people to accomplish tasks, but they neglect the essential role of developing leaders. In many cases, staff members are under enormous stress. They have a long list of jobs that need to be done—and done now!—and they're desperate for help. They are thrilled and relieved when someone steps into the gap to complete a task, but they don't even think about developing the person as a leader. We'll never have truly healthy cultures, however, if we don't identify and develop a host of strong, creative, passionate leaders.

Team leaders need to be perceptive about how rising leaders are assimilated into the group. Are old leaders threatened, or do they celebrate and mentor the new people? Great organizations enlist existing leaders to be part of the leadership pipeline, encouraging them to offer their insights and expertise and to help young leaders in every possible way.

Take a Look

+ How would you describe the leadership pipeline in your organization?

+ How well is the system working in identifying and developing rising leaders?

+ What kinds of resources (time, money, personnel, and so on) are devoted to leadership development?

+ When times are tough, what happens to leadership development in your organization?

Trust

Mutual trust among team members is the glue that makes everything good possible. Without it, a team quickly disintegrates into a gang of people protecting their turf and forming angry alliances. Trust is important up, down, and across the organizational structure. People need to have confidence that their supervisors mean what they say and say what they mean. When people trust each other, they make a strong connection between the vision, their own roles, the input of others, strategic planning, and the steps of implementation.

Trust may be freely given, but it is usually earned as people watch each other respond in good times and bad. Integrity and consistency provide a firm foundation for relationships to thrive. Trust is fluid. It takes time to be built, but it can be destroyed

> Trust grows in an environment that is HOT: honest, open, and transparent.

in an instant. Trust grows in an environment that is HOT: honest, open, and transparent. People aren't expected to be perfect, but they are expected to own their failures as well as their successes. Confession, contrary to popular opinion, is good both for the soul *and* for the person's reputation.

Failure and times of difficulty are the windows people use to determine if others are genuinely trustworthy. It's easy to put on a happy face when times are good, but struggles reveal a person's true nature. In hard times for an individual, the team, or the church, the hearts of everyone on the team are exposed. When others fail in an important task, do the leader and team members delight in pouncing on the person who blew it, or do they use the failure as an opportunity for growth? And the person who failed isn't the only one who notices how he's being treated. Everyone on the team is watching; all members are living the experience vicariously, anticipating how they'll be treated when they fail.

Office gossip is one of the most prevalent—and one of the most destructive—behaviors for many teams. Gossip, I believe, isn't innocent fun. It's a form of undercover revenge designed to harm someone. In an article on workplace gossip, Shayla McKnight reports that she joined a company that had a no-gossip policy. She explains, "At the beginning of my employment interview two years ago, Marne Reed, the human resources manager who interviewed me, mentioned the company's no-gossip policy. She said something like this: 'There's no back-stabbing here, and no office politics. Gossiping and talking behind someone's back are not tolerated.' I remember thinking: 'Really? That's odd. How is that possible?' Everywhere I've worked people have gossiped." She says that the environment at this company is different because of the policy: "There's a greater sense of being part of a team here than in other jobs I've had. If employees do violate the company policy, a manager speaks to them, and if they don't stop, they're let go. It might be human nature to think an unkind thought about a co-worker, but it's a choice whether or not to actually say it."[3]

Trust can be shattered in an instant by a dramatic event, or, more often, it is slowly eroded by countless relatively small but abrasive comments and actions. Every team is made up of flawed human beings, so on every team, trust will be an issue to some degree at some time with someone. Depending on the situation, it doesn't have to ruin a team. In fact, relationships that rebuild broken trust often are stronger and healthier than ever before because the people involved had to be ruthlessly honest, find forgiveness, and communicate better than before.

Take a Look

+ In what ways is trust being built or eroded on your team?

+ How does creating a HOT (honest, open, and transparent) environment build trust? In what ways does it threaten people?

+ How is failure treated on your team? How does that response affect the level of trust?

+ How does the team handle gossip? Are there clear guidelines? Should there be some? Why or why not?

Unafraid

Corporate courage is an incredibly appealing but slippery trait. I marvel at the bravery of soldiers who face withering enemy fire and mind-numbing conditions, but keep pressing forward until they win the battle. What is the source of their courage? It's not the absence of fear. They face a host of doubts and terrors, but soldiers report that two things keep them going: a clear conviction of the nobility of their cause and a commitment to the men fighting next to them. As I've watched church teams over the years, I've seen the same pattern. They aren't fighting a battle against flesh and blood, but men and women on staff teams face difficulties and challenges with courage if, and only if, they are convinced that what they are doing counts for all eternity and they believe in the people serving on their team.

Too often, I've met with teams who had a staff member or two who felt they had to walk on eggshells instead of speaking out boldly. For some reason (and it could be any of a host of issues, usually stemming from a painful past, but sometimes more recent wounds in the team environment), they feel insecure, and they believe they need to hide to avoid any risk. Being wrong or being asked a hard question, they assume, is the worst possible fate.

> Great leaders welcome dissenting opinions, as long as they are offered in good will and with an eye toward a solution.

Healthy teams foster the perspective that failure isn't a tragedy and conflict isn't the end of the world. Great leaders welcome dissenting opinions, as long as they are offered in good will and with an eye toward a solution. These teams are willing to take great risks and even to fail miserably because they've gotten over the notion that failure is a personal flaw. They believe that God is worthy of noble efforts, and they trust that God smiles on them as they attempt great things for him. When they look at one another, they don't see competitors; they see friends who have their backs as they take big risks. Courage, support, and innovation go hand in hand in inspiring cultures.

Take a Look

+ What are some examples of courage on your team in the past year or so?

+ How does one person's courage affect a team? How do defensiveness and timidity affect it?

+ Why is it important that wisdom direct a person's courage? What happens when a person is courageous without being wise?

+ In what ways is courage "caught, not taught"?

Responsive

Teams with healthy cultures are alert to open doors and ones that are closing. An individual may not notice a particular threat or opportunity, but someone else on the team will. These teams develop the productive habit of keeping their eyes open so that they can handle every situation: on the team, in individuals' lives, in the church family, and in the community.

For teams to be responsive, they have to develop a consistent process for collaboration, with communication lines that are wide open. They value analysis and feedback, and they work on becoming and staying aligned with one another. Infighting and turf wars steal people's attention and keep them from noticing and responding to the needs around them. Effective teams, though, work hard to keep their minds and hearts focused on God's purposes. After decisions are made, team members fully support the team's decision. They understand that an individual's foot-dragging or resistance can hold up the entire process, so they learn the art of communication and finding common ground. They publicly support the team's decision instead of lobbying in the hallway for their contrarian's point of view for days or weeks.

Responsive teams don't just focus on big goals and sweeping strategies. They develop the habit of taking care of the little things, such as promptly returning phone calls, responding to e-mails, and communicating decisions to everyone who needs to know when he or she needs to know it.

Strong, vibrant cultures don't allow silos to close off communication between teams. In a somewhat whimsical but accurate definition of the term, a "business dictionary" says that silos in organizations are "non-communication between departments, incompatible goal-setting, intra-company snobbery, or out-right hostility. The term refers to the sealed-off nature of silos rather than to their utility in storing tomorrow's breakfast cereal. At

> The larger the organization grows, the greater the amount of energy that needs to be invested in being responsive to people inside and outside the team.

its most extreme, siloing in the workplace leads to destructive competition among nominal allies while providing an opportunity to abuse agricultural metaphors."[4]

Leaders in healthy cultures work hard to disseminate information among the departments and get buy-in up and down the chain of command and between teams. Being responsive requires both a sensitive spirit and a workable system to make sure things don't fall through the cracks. The larger the organization grows, the greater the amount of energy that needs to be invested in being responsive to people inside and outside the team.

Take a Look

+ How responsive is your team to threats and opportunities? What are the signs of responsiveness (or lack of it)?

+ How do collaboration and communication affect a team's responsiveness?

+ How often do "little things" like returning phone calls and e-mails fall through the cracks on your team? Is this a problem? Why or why not?

+ Does your team's current organizational system (delegation, feedback, collaboration, and so on) foster responsiveness or hinder it? Explain your answer.

Execution

In my conversations with leaders and team members, one of their chief concerns is that teams often talk about decisions but fail to follow through on implementing them. When they don't see the fruit of their discussions, they lose faith in each other and become discouraged. It's not a big deal if something doesn't get done because someone was sick or there's another good excuse, but systemwide, consistent failure poisons the atmosphere. Executing decisions is a function of clarity, roles and responsibilities, and the system of accountability.

To be sure that follow-through becomes the norm, leaders need to define goals very clearly. Decisions should be articulated with precision, including who, what, why, when, where, and how. Obviously, some decisions require more thought and precision than others, but many teams err on the side of fogginess, and the team suffers.

Clear delegation is essential to execution. The person responsible needs to understand her authority and how to relate to everyone else involved. This person should walk out of the meeting with crystal-clear expectations, a plan to coordinate with others, deadlines, and any other requirements.

On some teams, accountability is haphazard at best, but this breeds complacency even among those who would normally be conscientious about following through with their commitments. People don't do what we expect; they do what we inspect. Plans are worthless unless they have target goals, deadlines, access to resources, and a budget. With those things in place, the leader needs to ask for regular updates on progress. She can ask in any way that works: e-mail, phone calls, personal appointments, or, even better, in the staff meetings. Asking for progress reports in meetings lets the whole team know how progress is being made and the role members might play in helping the person complete the plan. Some people mistakenly believe that deadlines aren't very important, but they are the benchmark that keeps a plan on track.

To help leaders plan and delegate more effectively, I suggest that they use a simple planning template and that they train their staff to use it too. (See the template in Appendix 2.)

Developing a culture of accountability takes the mystery and the sting out of giving reports. If everybody is asked to report, then nobody is singled out. If, however, someone consistently fails to follow through, the leader can recognize it more quickly if the system is in place, and she can help the person clarify the goals, develop skills, find resources, or overcome any other challenge that has prevented him from taking steps toward execution.

To facilitate clear, accurate reporting from team members on the tasks they've been assigned, I suggest that teams use a simple reporting grid. (See Appendix 3 for a sample.) In a culture that executes plans well, the leader is committed to ongoing training to equip team members to achieve the highest goals. Incompetent people are retrained, moved to roles that fit them better, or removed from the team. The organization is committed to ensuring that people are serving in roles that match their strengths. Leaders focus on these strengths, not on people's weaknesses, and they pursue excellence in every aspect of corporate life, including communication and team building. A relentless pursuit of excellence in execution is a catalyst—not a hindrance—for healthy relationships.

Take a Look

+ At the end of each staff meeting, how clearly defined are the goals and responsibilities of each person? How do you know?

+ How are people held accountable on your team?

+ How do team members give feedback to each other about their performance and communication?

+ How would you describe the blend of heart motivation and the pursuit of excellence on your team?

Getting Buy-in

One person can change the composition of a team. It's best if the leader grasps the importance of creating an inspiring culture and takes bold steps with the team, but a wise, tenacious team member can begin to create this kind of environment.

I've seen some leaders try to change their organizations by fiat, demanding that people trust each other, communicate freely, and be more responsive to those inside and outside the team. But as you can imagine, these efforts only further eroded the environment and created one more hurdle to overcome. Great leaders put cultural issues on the table and invite honest, open, and transparent conversations about changing the atmosphere. They know it's going to take time, and they are willing to lead the process. They understand, though, that a successful transition of a team's culture depends on the buy-in of each person on the team—and perhaps the replacement of those who prove unwilling to take steps of progress. Building a great team involves everybody, and in fact it works most effectively when team members feel empowered to give input, develop strategies, and take steps in shaping the culture. In an interview about his organizational culture, Steve Ellis, worldwide managing director of Bain & Company, explained, "If you're looking for a little management philosophy, then my advice is to keep cultural initiatives organic and driven by the employees, with a little support from management.…Top-down cultural mandates simply don't work." Developing a powerfully positive culture, though, isn't just about people feeling good about themselves and each other. Production matters. Ellis reports, "Results serve as the core of our culture. We are passionate about what we do, enjoy our work, laugh a lot, and celebrate success when we achieve it."[5]

Changing a culture requires tremendous patience. We can rearrange boxes on an organizational chart in a moment, but changing culture is heart surgery. Culture is not only *what* we do but also *why* and *how* we do it. Culture is about the heart and head, and then it shapes what we do with our hands. Leaders also need a healthy dose of creativity as they take their teams through cultural change. In an article on teamwork, Keith Sawyer, a researcher at Washington University in St. Louis, describes the impact of "group genius," the ability of a team to work together to apply creative insights. He says, "Innovation today isn't a sudden break with the past, a brilliant insight that one lone outsider pushes through to save the business. Just the opposite: innovation today is a continuous process of small and constant change, and it's built into the culture of successful businesses."[6]

> Culture is about the heart and head, and then it shapes what we do with our hands.

Cultural transformation may begin when an individual has a fresh insight about the need to work together more effectively, but sooner or later, everyone on the team has to get involved in the process. Some jump on the wagon with enthusiasm; others are brought along more reluctantly—but everyone on the team has to become a willing partner in the venture. When people bring their best to the team, amazing things can happen. As the Japanese proverb says, "None of us is as smart as all of us."

Think About It . . .

1. As you looked at the keys of CULTURE in this chapter, in which area is your team doing well? What is the area that needs the most attention?

2. What is your role in changing and shaping your team's culture?

3. What will it take to get buy-in from the whole team? What will you have to overcome? What resources will you need?

Use the questions in each section of the CULTURE analysis with your team to open dialogue, stimulate discussion, and gain objectivity about the current culture of the team.

For a free CULTURE survey for you and your team, go to www.samchandculturesurvey.com.

VOCABULARY DEFINES CULTURE

When you have healthy supervisors and good working conditions, what more do workers look for?...There is really only one answer to this question: Recognition. Not just bonuses and plaques, privileged parking spaces or "worker of the week" announcements, though these are very important, but the type of recognition that affirms the value of your self at the deepest possible level.

—Dr. Archibald Hart

When I was in the first grade in India, I was a rambunctious kid. I remember stepping from desk to desk across the room. I'm sure I exasperated my teacher, Miss Boniface. One day, she looked at me as I was walking across the desks and sighed, "Samuel, you are just a *janvar*." In Hindi, the word means "animal." I'm sure she didn't mean any harm. She wasn't yelling or clenching her teeth at me, but for the rest of my years in that elementary school, the name stuck. From that day on, students and teachers called me janvar, and I lived up to my moniker. The word defined me and gave me an identity. I acted like an animal because that's what people expected of me, and I spent many hours in the principal's office. I didn't devote myself to being a good scholar, and I didn't spend my energies on sports. I picked fights every day. I never won a fight—not one. In fights, I scraped, clawed, bit, and kicked. The fights really never ended because I started them again the next day. In fact, I fought with the same people day after day all year. My life revolved around being as disruptive as I could be so that I could validate others' opinion of me. Everybody wants to be known for something, and acting like an animal immediately became my USP—my unique selling point.

But words can also have a wonderful, inspiring effect. Many years later, I had shed my identity as an animal to become an academician. I was president of Beulah Heights University, and I had learned to be effective at administration, vision casting, and building relationships. One day, however, a man I respected looked me in the eye and said, "Sam, you are a really good leader." To be honest, I was very surprised by his comment because I had never seen myself as a leader. My curriculum in Bible college and seminary didn't have a single course on leadership, and I wasn't even sure what a leader was. I knew, though, that this statement had the potential to change my life. This man's sincere affirmation meant the world to me, and the fact that he qualified the word "leader" with "really good" gave me a new standard to live up to. From that day, I saw my role in a different light. It wasn't that I changed directions or careers, but now I viewed myself and my role through a broader lens, and I had confidence that God could use me in bigger ways. My friend hadn't made an appointment that day to tell me how he saw me, and he wasn't playing the role of a life coach or mentor. He was just a trusted friend who held up a mirror to affirm what he saw in me, and he encouraged me deeply.

> The words we use, and the way we use them, define organizational culture.

Words have the power to shape lives and organizations. Too often, however, leaders aren't aware of their vocabulary as they speak, and they don't realize how people are affected by their words. Even casually spoken statements can have profound effects. The words we use, and the way we use them, define organizational culture. Some leaders think that the vocabulary of culture is only about painting the biggest, most dramatic vision they can paint—the bigger the better. But that's not the case. Vision statements are only a small part of the vocabulary of a culture. Factors that are just as important include:

+ Avoiding terms that actually hinder us from fulfilling God's vision

+ Using informal, compassionate conversations to show empathy and build trust

+ Occasionally stopping in the middle of a meeting to talk about how the team is communicating

+ Being honest with team members and avoiding "happy talk"

+ Learning to listen with our hearts, eyes, and ears

+ Speaking words of genuine affirmation

+ Intentionally choosing vocabulary to shape the culture

For most of us, the words we use are second nature. We don't even think about them anymore, but we can't overestimate the power of vocabulary to define culture. To make changes, we need honest reflection, feedback from the stakeholders at every level, and the courage to change not only our words but also our hearts as we speak them.

Every Industry Has a Vocabulary

Every field of study, every industry, and every organization creates its own vocabulary to communicate to its constituents. Insiders instantly recognize the meaning of words that may sound like a foreign language to outsiders. And in some fields, such as technology, vocabulary is changing at a rapid pace. The Word of the Year in 2005 was *podcast*, a term that today seems as though it's been around for decades. Auto repair shops, restaurants, the medical field, the energy industry, churches, theology, and all branches of business have developed (and continue to develop) a language that connects with its constituents. Our choice of words creates a bond among those who understand the meanings and context, but it also builds walls that keep out those who don't understand.

Vocabulary makes a difference in communicating at every level of a church's life: one-on-one, in teams, in departments, churchwide, and to the community. Too often, our language becomes exclusive—and even offensive—to people in the community we are trying to reach with the message of Christ. Our vision statements proclaim that we want to communicate God's love and forgiveness to those outside the family of God, but Joseph Mattera, presiding bishop of Christ Covenant Coalition and overseeing bishop of Resurrection Church in New York, observes that many churches have adopted word choices that "make new visitors uncomfortable." Mattera has seen visitors cringe or roll their eyes when church members use terms like "praise the Lord," "amen," or "hallelujah" in casual conversations. He concludes, "Until our church members understand how unchurched people view our services and rid them of unnecessary religious behavior, the Sunday morning experience will never attract multitudes of the unchurched, no matter how much soul winning is part of the vision of the church."[1]

The existing vocabulary in a church is seldom analyzed—and even less often challenged—because the choice of terms is ritualized in an airtight tradition. The culture around us is changing rapidly, and the language we use for some aspects of life is morphing almost daily, but many churches still use the same vocabulary they used decades (and even generations) ago. As the culture changes around us, we sound increasingly irrelevant.

The Language of Trust

Trust is the glue of any relationship, and authenticity is essential. When people get too busy to care for one another, trust erodes and defenses go up. Even though we are trying to reach every person on the planet, we need to slow down to show interest in each individual. A few days after someone has shared about her mother's illness, we can stop her in the hall and ask, "How's your mom doing? Is she feeling better?" We don't have to remember the details of the diagnosis, but our simple questions show her that we remember and that we care—and touch the heart of a worried friend.

When ministry leaders forget that their staff members are flesh-and-blood human beings and treat them as "production units," these leaders lose their voice to speak vision, direction, and challenge into others' lives. Small talk about the things that matter to people on our teams isn't small at all—it's enormously important. Most pastors enter the ministry because they love people, and they are gifted at the art of chitchat. They can talk to almost anybody at almost any time about almost anything. As the pressures of ministry compound, however, they tend to focus more on the administrative load and looming deadlines. Then every interaction becomes an organizational transaction instead of a relational connection. When we become bulldogs about the tasks and fail to take time to ask about a family member, a vacation, an illness, or a new haircut, people feel used, no matter how many checks we see on our agenda at the end of a meeting. Trust is built when we use inclusive instead of exclusive language: "I" instead of "you," "us" instead of "them," and "we" instead of "they." Obviously, sometimes we have to use words like "you," "them," and "they," but we need to watch the context and nuance of the message. For example, I've been in a staff meeting when someone said, "After *we* make this decision, *we* have to make sure that *they* understand what it means." The subtle implication was that the people in the room were the insiders and everyone else was an outsider. A better statement would be, "After this decision is made, we have to be sure that the whole team understands the implications." This wording implies that everyone is on the team, with equal value and equal status. This distinction matters to everyone. Those not in the meeting feel included as part of the team, and those in the meeting realize that there are no class divisions between insiders and outsiders. Does something so seemingly trivial really make a difference? Just ask people who feel excluded by the rest of their team.

When I was a university president, I discovered that the choice of words makes a big difference in attitudes and outcomes. At one point, we almost banned the word "problem" from our campus conversations because we noticed that it carried negative connotations. When people spoke of problems, they often had a sense of heaviness, even hopelessness, that was corrosive to the spirit of hope and faith. We consciously substituted the word "challenge," and we noticed that people instinctively sensed that people rise to meet challenges. Soon, the culture of our school changed from slightly negative to distinctly positive—all because we chose to use a different vocabulary.

As staff teams grow larger with multiple layers of leadership, I'm afraid that some churches are losing some of the magic of the vocabulary of volunteers. In the business community and with paid staff, we feel that we can demand compliance because people pick up a paycheck every couple of weeks. We can say, "The meeting tomorrow starts at 9:00 a.m. Don't be late." The subtle (or not so subtle) message is that the person will be in deep trouble if he doesn't show up on time. But with volunteers, we know we don't have that kind of leverage, so we appeal to "the better angels" of their natures. We take a little more time to explain the importance of the meeting and the contribution they'll make when they come. Then, when we say to the volunteer exactly the same thing we said to the paid staff member, "The meeting tomorrow starts at 9:00 a.m. Don't be late," the person hears it as an invitation to be part of something that will change people's lives! An honest analysis of the vocabulary of our church cultures involves looking at how we motivate our staff and volunteers. Sadly, too many churches treat volunteers like paid staff and demand compliance with precious little heart motivation. Instead, we need to treat staff like volunteers, always appealing to their hearts and their desire for God to use them to change lives. Some will ask, "But what about accountability?" If we're asking people to

> We need to treat staff like volunteers, always appealing to their hearts and their desire for God to use them to change lives.

join us in touching lives and changing people's eternal destinies and they aren't excited about it, we may have one of two problems: we may have picked the wrong people, so we need to replace them, or we may not be connecting the vision with their hearts. When the right people are placed properly and invited to make a difference for the kingdom, accountability is seldom a problem—and it should never be a primary means of motivating people, whether they are staff or volunteers.

The culture of a team is shaped by the dominant person, who may not necessarily be the one with the title who sits at the head of the table. This person may be an enthusiastic, charismatic team member who expresses optimism that the team can accomplish even the most difficult challenge, but more often, it's a surly, opinionated person who feels compelled to voice every objection under the sun. The dominant person either demands to be the power broker or steps into a void left by an ineffective leader. Soon, the vocabulary used by the dominant person becomes the collective language of the team.

Quite often, people on a team have very different "hot button" issues they want to champion, so the dominant person may change from issue to issue. One person may feel strongly about the way printed material is presented to the congregation, so she lobbies with passion for excellence in these pieces. Another person couldn't care less about brochures and other handouts, but he wants the team to do something significant about the homeless in the community. The list of interests is almost endless, and for each one, team members may lobby for the team's participation and resources, sometimes with reason and eloquence; sometimes demanding compliance from others; and sometimes with joyful enthusiasm, inviting team members to join together in making a difference. Look for the language of each topic's champion. Notice how each person promotes his or her issue, and observe the response of the team members.

Starting Strong

The first thirty to forty-five seconds of a meeting are crucial. Most leaders, however, don't think much about how people are introduced to the meeting and the message of the day. When I have the remote control to my television in my hand and I'm flipping through channels to find something interesting to watch, I give each channel only two or three seconds to capture my interest. When we sit down at a conference table, the people in the room don't give us much more time than that. If we don't grab their hearts in those first few seconds, their minds will drift to other things they have quickly concluded are more important than our less-than-compelling agenda. And again, vocabulary is important. I've walked into a meeting when the leader announced, "I'm not sure what we need to do today," and the disinterest in the room was almost palpable. I've also heard a leader begin a meeting by saying, "A lot of people have told me that they disagreed with our decision." Immediately, I realized I had to guess who he was talking about, and I didn't want to play a guessing game. I wanted the cold, hard facts, with the issue stated as a challenge the team could overcome as they marshal their collective resources to meet it. A better way to begin the meeting is to say, "Last Thursday, I met with Larry (who, everyone knows, is a major donor), and he has some questions about the direction of the youth ministry." I may not agree with Larry's assessment of the situation, but I respect Larry as a key member of the church. The vocabulary used in this first sentence captures my attention and piques my interest.

Make the first statement positive instead of negative, inclusive instead of exclusive, and hopeful instead of complaining about the past.

As leaders we need to carefully plan the first couple of sentences for every meeting we lead. Very simply, a good beginning can say something like, "What we are talking about in this meeting has implications for the way the community perceives our church (or how we develop leaders, or anything else that's important to the team). This meeting is crucial, and we need everyone's help." Leaders have only a few seconds to connect with people in the room and enlist their participation in the discussion. Make the first statement positive instead of negative, inclusive instead of exclusive, and hopeful instead of complaining about the past. A few minutes of preparation equip us to begin well, and those first moments work wonders to grab people's hearts and set the tone for the rest of the meeting.

Asides

As we prepare for meetings and carefully choose our vocabulary for the first few sentences, we can anticipate who on the team will be the "yes, but" people and who will be the "yes, and" people. One of our jobs as leaders is to give some power to those who will carry the ball down the field and to gently nudge the negative people to see problems as challenges. Identifying these people doesn't take a doctorate in psychology. We've seen team members respond in dozens of meetings before, and we can accurately predict how they'll respond this time.

A leader's feedback about team members' contributions in a meeting is just as important as the discussion itself. These brief interludes and reflections are "asides" that guide group members' perceptions of how they are working together. In many meetings, I stop and reflect on a person who has made a valuable contribution. I may say something to the group like, "Did you notice what just happened in our discussion?" Then I'll turn to the individual and say, "Bill, you helped us move the conversation forward when you asked an insightful question, listened carefully, and then offered a solution. Could you tell how your contribution affected our meeting? I sure noticed, and I want you to know that I appreciate your impact today."

Asides aren't always glowingly positive. Sometimes, honest feedback can serve the dual purposes of correction and inspiration. When I noticed that Mary was always voicing concerns and shooting down constructive ideas, I stopped the meeting and said, "Mary, let me give you some feedback about how you influence the group. I've noticed that you have very good insights about the challenges we face, and you articulate them very well, but I haven't seen you offer many constructive solutions. That's important, too." Then I turn to the team and tell them, "Let's make this a standard for our team: let's be very frank about the challenges we face,

> The process of the conversation is just as important (and ultimately, even more important) than the immediate topic of the conversation.

but when we bring up something in the group, let's also offer at least three possible solutions to discuss. And now, let's get back to the point we were discussing." Mary knows that I haven't targeted her behavior alone for correction; we've made a commitment as a team to be rigorously honest and solution oriented. The message to the group is that the leader is aware not only of the issue being discussed but also of the way each group member is framing that issue. The process of the conversation is just as important (and ultimately, even more important) than the immediate topic of the conversation.

Leaders shouldn't use asides too often, or they will be accused of psychoanalyzing team members. A few times a year is enough, but those times leave a powerful impression on each person on the team. Sometimes I plan an aside before the meeting ever begins. For instance, I've walked into a meeting and told the group,

> Before we get into our agenda for today, I want to give you some feedback about some patterns I've noticed in our discussions in the past few weeks. It seems that we talk about the issues, but I don't think we're putting 100 percent of our ideas and hearts on the table. The reason I say this is that in the past few weeks, several of you have told me things after we met that could have been shared in the meeting. And in fact, those comments would have changed our decisions in the meetings. I'm confused about why you don't feel like you can say those things when we meet as a team. Can you help me with this?

I may pause to see if anyone volunteers an answer. If no one does, I may say,

> Of course, I don't know the answer, but here are some possible reasons. You may not trust one or more people in the group, or

maybe you aren't sure how to handle it when people disagree. I want to assure you that it's perfectly okay for us to disagree as long as we do it agreeably. Maybe you aren't confident that you'll have all the answers if people ask you a question. That's fine, too. You can always say, "Good question. I'll get back to you on that." Here's the reason I'm bringing this up today: when you bring me additional information after we've made a collective decision, I second-guess our first decision, and I wonder if we're giving people everything we can. I don't want to do an 80 percent job for our people, and I know you don't want to either. Do any of these things ring a bell for you? Tell me what you're thinking.

And then I listen. Quite often, people voice personal inhibitions and surface things that happened long ago on other church staff teams. They've brought their fears to our team. Or maybe someone on the team has offended another, and trust has been strained. They don't want to take any risk of being vulnerable in front of the other, so they pull back and protect themselves. There may be any of dozens of reasons, but shining a light on the team's process of communication provides an opportunity to speak openly about our fears, hurts, and hopes so that trust can be rebuilt.

The Gift of Honesty

One of the most valuable things we can give people on our teams is the gift of honesty. People instinctively know if a leader is holding back information, shading the truth, or expressing blind optimism. Happy talk may be intended to look like genuine faith in God, but it comes across as phony, and a lack of authenticity poisons a team. The beginning point, though, isn't for the leader to simply analyze word choices. It's deeper than that. The first task is to take a long, hard look at the difference between respecting people and manipulating them. The two are polar opposites. When we respect someone, we value her as a person, and we honor her opinions even if we disagree with her. When a leader's agenda is to control people to get them to believe "the right way" and do "the right things," he's engaged in manipulation, not true leadership. In the article "How to Talk Straight in Hard Times," management consultants Maren and Jamie Showkeir observe, "One of the most powerful—and underutilized—ways to [engage employees] is through managing conversations instead of 'managing others.' How leaders talk to people matters, and authentic conversations create cultures where the survival, prosperity, and success of the organization is everybody's business."[2] The Showkeirs equate "managing others" with manipulating them. When people feel pressured to conform to our desires or direction, we may have slipped over into the realm of manipulation. Respecting people who have different opinions is essential if we want to create an inspiring culture.

The gift of honesty begins not with words but with the leader's perception and intentions. When we feel stressed, threatened, or out of control, our instinctive response is "fight or flight." We become defensive and demanding, and our goal changes from leading people to controlling them. In a flash or over a long period, we shift from treating them like adults to treating them like small children. When we play the role of "benevolent parents," we feel justified in telling them only part of the truth, and we protect our position as the keepers of reality. We may have seen people on our teams worry or explode when they learned painful information, and we want to avoid that response again at all costs—perhaps because we interpret their negative response as a reflection on our leadership. First, then, we need to be honest with ourselves about how we view people on our teams. Do we respect them as adults and thus can be honest with them, or do we believe we need to treat them like children and filter the information we share with them?

When we determine to treat people as adults, we then have some choices about our vocabulary. We can use the word "challenge" instead of "problem," but we need to be bluntly honest about the size of the hill that the team needs to climb. People may not like what they hear, but they respect leaders who speak the unvarnished truth.

Authenticity requires another step, however. If we want to create a culture of trust on our teams, leaders also need to acknowledge any personal faults in communicating with the team and the harm they have done. One ministry leader told his team, "During the last few months when we've been under a lot of stress with the reorganization, I realized I haven't been the leader you need me to be. Instead of treating you like adults and telling you the truth, I've hidden some things from you. I think you sensed that, and I can tell that you don't trust me as much as you used to. I take responsibility for that, and I'm sorry. I can give lots of excuses, but good intentions aren't good enough. Will you forgive me?" After they responded, he continued, "I promise I'll do whatever it takes for us to have healthy relationships, and I'll tell you the truth. I want you to be a part of the solution, and if I don't tell you the truth, you can't be. What do you think about what I've said today?"

> When team members share their hearts, especially hurtful things, the leader needs to listen carefully without a shred of defensiveness.

His last question invited people on the team to share their frustration, anger, and disappointment. The leader may not want to hear these comments, but they are the path of healing and hope for the future of the team. When team members share their hearts, especially hurtful things, the leader needs to listen carefully without a shred of defensiveness. One of the most important statements a leader can make during these conversations is actually a question: "Would you tell me more about that?" This simple question shows that he welcomes the team member's honest feedback.

When people have shared their frustrations and the tank of disappointment has run dry, the leader can express hope that the future will be different. His commitment is, "From now on, I'll treat you with respect. I promise. And if you ever feel that I'm trying to manipulate you, I give you permission to tell me. I assure you that I'll listen. Can we make that commitment to each other?" The leader's promise and invitation provide a strong foundation for the future of the team, but the original organizational challenge hasn't gone away. It's still a steep hill for the team to climb. The leader needs to state the challenge objectively, without promising "everything will work out just fine." That's just happy talk. A more accurate and more reassuring statement would be, "We face a tough challenge, but I'm sure God has some purposes in it for all of us. Let's tackle it together."

To make sure there are no hidden agendas and unaddressed emotional baggage, I developed a habit of ending meetings by going around the room and asking each person, "Is there anything you haven't said to me that you need to say or want to say?" Sometimes people seize the opportunity to say, "Yes, I have a concern that I want you to know about." And we take some time to address it there. This lets people know that I care about what they care about, but this practice has an additional value. It lets each person know that she has an open invitation to bring up her perspectives and concerns throughout the meeting, and if they don't come up in the course of conversation, she can voice them at the end. People's concerns are always important to me. Another benefit of this approach is that it normalizes honesty in the context of the group. Group members know that it's not acceptable to avoid important topics in the group and then talk to me later. If something is important to the group's process and decisions, members need to bring it up in the group.

The vocabulary of honesty can be spoken only by a leader who has made a commitment to respect people on the team. Manipulation, even with the best of intentions, may bring short-term gains of lowering tension for the moment, but it eventually causes

> Respect, honesty, responsibility, and hope are the language of a great team leader.

people to feel devalued, and they conclude that the leader isn't a person they want to follow. Respect, honesty, responsibility, and hope are the language of a great team leader.

Questions and Slouching

Never in all of history has communication been so immediate and accessible, but I'm afraid the technological advances have had the unintended consequence of eroding the art of listening. The proliferation of devices has changed the way we relate. We expect to stay connected to everyone and everything through our cell phones, PDAs, text messaging, e-mail, and the Internet. Linda Stone, formerly of Apple and Microsoft, coined the term *continuous partial attention* to describe the constant distractions of our communication devices. She reports,

> To pay continuous partial attention is to pay partial attention—CONTINUOUSLY. It is motivated by a desire to be a LIVE node on the network. Another way of saying this is that we want to connect and be connected. We want to effectively scan for opportunity and optimize for the best opportunities, activities, and contacts, in any given moment. To be busy, to be connected, is to be alive, to be recognized, and to matter. We pay continuous partial attention in an effort NOT TO MISS ANYTHING. It is an always-on, anywhere, anytime, any place behavior that involves an artificial sense of constant crisis. We are always in high alert when we pay continuous partial attention. This artificial sense of constant crisis is more typical of continuous partial attention than it is of multi-tasking.[3]

To change the way we communicate with people so that we genuinely connect with them instead of just passing on information, we can do two simple but profound things to enhance listening: ask pertinent questions and use the power of slouching. People get tired in meetings if they feel that they're being *talked to* but not invited to *talk with* the rest of the team. Let me share a few ideas that I've found effective:

+ Attention spans are getting shorter and shorter, so we need to keep people engaged by asking for their input. A simple question, "What do you think?" can work wonders. It's become a staple in the way I lead meetings because I've seen a simple question stimulate people and keep them actively involved.

+ I can tell if people are listening to me if they ask follow-up questions. If there are none, I assume they were just asking for my input because they have to, not because they are genuinely interested in what I have to say.

+ When someone has shared a point of view, I often say, "That's a good point. Will you tell us more about that?" Or I invite him to be more explicit: "I've never seen it that way. Explain how it works in a little more detail."

+ When I don't understand what someone is saying, I don't bark, "That makes absolutely no sense to me. What in the world are you talking about?" Instead, I sit back and explore: "That's an intriguing point of view. Help me understand what you're saying."

+ Quite often, after listening to someone explain a point of view, I ask the group for their feedback, "Suzie told us her perspective. What do you think about what she told us?" Almost always, others in the group give valuable feedback to highlight the strong points and expose weaknesses. As the leader, I then don't have to fix every problem and answer every question. The group functions effectively as a team, and I'm not forced to function as a benevolent dictator.

Asking for additional input takes a little longer, but we have to understand the goal of our meetings. If the goal is to check off all the boxes on an arbitrary list of items, then by all means, press forward and charge through the list. But if the goal is to enflame the hearts of people and enlist their passionate involvement in the process, then we need to slow down and involve them more deeply in the conversation by asking for their contributions. Of course, taking time to ask for input, listen carefully, and value discussion about a finite list of topics doesn't leave time for other things that could have been discussed. The leader's role is then to be the CPO, the chief priority officer. Many times I've had to say, "We had some important things that we didn't get to talk about today, but we need to address these topics." If the issue is pertinent to only one or two of the group members, I sometimes ask them to meet with me between group meetings so that we can discuss it and move forward. If the topic concerns all of us, I usually ask everyone to think about it and bring some suggestions when we meet next time. They need to know that we will address important topics, but we need to be flexible and prepared so that we use our time wisely. When individuals and teams are confident, they feel free to fully engage the situation and each other. I call this "dancing in the moment."

Many of us feel that we have to settle every disagreement before we can move on, so we avoid disagreements—especially with people who have a history of being sour or demanding. An important principle of creating a healthy culture is becoming comfortable with some unresolved issues. A leader can say, "I can tell that we disagree about this, and I don't think we're going to resolve it now. Let's think about it and talk again next week. I want to ask each of you to bring a possible solution when we talk again." With this mind-set, we can ask for input without demanding universal agreement and instant compliance.

> An important principle of creating a healthy culture is becoming comfortable with some unresolved issues.

Many oral communicators aren't good listeners, and people who feel pressured by deadlines and long to-do lists often are preoccupied with phone calls, texts, and e-mails during a meeting instead of making eye contact and listening to people with their hearts, eyes, and ears. These distracted behaviors communicate loudly and clearly: "You're not important to me!" Listening, though, isn't just about getting the facts. Nonverbal communication is very important, especially when we're listening. When I'm leading a team or meeting with an individual, I often employ "the power of slouching." I push my chair away from the table, sit back, cross my legs, and turn to face the person who is speaking so as to make eye contact. These actions send a powerful message: "I care about you and what you have to say, and I'm not in a hurry for you finish. Take your time and give me your best input." Giving people our undivided, relaxed attention lets them know that we are listening with our minds, our hearts, and our eyes, as well as with our ears. They feel that they are important and that we value them as people, not just as interchangeable cogs in the organizational machine.

"Some People"

One of the guidelines in building authentic relationships is to avoid vague accusations. Years ago, I spent far too much time chasing rabbits when someone in a group reported, "*Some people* have a problem with this or that." We tried to guess who it was, and we tried to address the problem even though the person who reported it was intentionally vague to protect his sources. Fairly soon, I realized this had to change, so I told the group, "We won't bring up any reports or complaints unless we identify the person who told us. If you don't have the person's permission to tell us, then don't make the report."

Years ago when I was a pastor in Michigan, a man in our church died, and we expected a lot of people to come to the funeral. In those days before e-mail and text messaging, we did the best we could to get the word out about the time and place of the funeral. At a board meeting about a week after the funeral, a member of our board announced, "Some people were upset that they didn't get the word about the funeral. They wanted to come, but they didn't hear about it in time."

I told him, "Joe, you know we don't talk about complaints unless we have the names of the people. If you'll tell us, we'll address it."

He didn't want to tell us who the person was (this was our first clue that it was an individual, not "some people"), so he remained quiet. I could tell, however, that he was agitated. At the end of the meeting, I asked if anyone had anything they wanted to tell me that hadn't come up, and Joe blurted out, "Okay, I'll tell you. It was Mr. Richardson. He was really upset that nobody told him about the funeral." Then, with genuine anger, he snorted, "And to be honest, I don't blame him."

As soon as the last word left Joe's lips, two board members told him that they had personally communicated with Mr. Richardson on the day of the death. One had seen him in the store, and the other left a message in his mailbox. If the accusation had remained nebulous and anonymous, the issue would have taken too much time in our discussions, and we almost certainly would have come to some wrong conclusions. This was an important cultural lesson for me, for our board, and especially for Joe.

I don't read anonymous letters. I tear them up and discard them. Anonymous people are cowards.

The principle of dealing with specifics instead of vague generalities also applies to how team members talk about the leader. People talk about their leaders—it's human nature—but they need to be taught that authenticity works both ways. They need to speak honestly with their leaders if they have concerns about their leadership. Years ago, I found out that a man on our board had been talking to several people to complain about my leadership. I saw this as an important moment to shape the atmosphere of our board, so at the next meeting, I addressed him in front of the group: "John, I understand that you said certain things to particular people about me. I'm not interested in finding out what you said or the list of people you talked to. That's not important to me. What I want to know is, what is it about our relationship and the context of our board meetings that prevented you from talking with me here? You had ample opportunity to do so, but you chose not to." I didn't want to become a detective to uncover what he said to whom. The only important issue was my relationship with him and the value of authenticity among us on the board. I could have talked to him outside the group, but I saw it as a cultural issue, not a personal one. And although my initial question was to the individual, my question was about the whole group: What is it about

> To build a new culture, we first had to recognize and destroy the old one—not destroy the person, but destroy the culture of suspicion and secret alliances.

our relationships, our honesty, and our care for one another that needs attention?

The conversation among us that day was one of the richest and most significant we ever had as a board. If I had let John's gossiping go on, I would have given tacit permission to everyone to talk outside the group instead of in the group about the things that matter most: trust, respect, and honesty. To build a new culture, however, we first had to recognize and destroy the old one— not destroy the person, but destroy the culture of suspicion and secret alliances. Actually, the issue of the man complaining to his friends only kick-started the conversation about our board's culture. After my initial statement, I didn't address him directly. He looked sheepish as the discussion developed, and he didn't add a lot to the give-and-take, but I'm sure he learned a valuable lesson that day.

Consistency

People on staff and volunteer teams watch their leaders like a hawk, and they want to see consistency between their words and their actions. A friend of mine told me about the leader of a national ministry who presented himself as a kind, wise, compassionate man of God, but behind closed doors, he was demanding and severely critical of anyone who dared voice a dissenting view. Soon his staff members were divided into the loyalists who turned a blind eye to his incongruent behavior, and the dissenters whose frustration and disrespect created enormous tension in their own lives and their relationships in the organization. I've also known a few leaders whose public and private personas were reversed. They were as kind and loving as a mother with the people in their offices and boardrooms, but when they spoke to the masses, they conveyed a raw anger that seemed far more than a righteous response to injustice.

As Abraham Lincoln famously said, "You can fool all of the people some of the time, and some of the people all of the time, but you can't fool all the people all the time." Followers notice the consistency of a leader's life. If his attitudes and behaviors in private match his public words of faith and nobility, they know they can trust him. If not, they first lose respect for the leader, then for their coworkers who remain loyal, and, finally, even for themselves for staying in such a toxic culture.

Thankfully, cases of significant inconsistency in churches and non-profit organizations are fairly rare. The ones that make the news capture our attention, but for every one of those, there are thousands of churches with competent, consistent leaders. To some degree, all leaders struggle with consistency because they have to balance vision for the future with compassion today

> Loyalty earned is a beautiful thing, but loyalty demanded is toxic.

for hurting people, but most find a way to live successfully in that tension. It's a wonderful thing when people report, "He's the same person in the lobby that he is in the pulpit, and he's the same in the committee meeting as he is in the hardware store." People thrive under this kind of leadership. Loyalty earned is a beautiful thing, but loyalty demanded is toxic.

Authentic Affirmation

When my friend told me years ago that he saw me as a "really good leader," his message was powerful because I could tell he meant it. For words of affirmation to be meaningful, they need to be specific, personal, and timely. I've heard many leaders say to almost anyone within earshot, "You're great!" That's a lot better than "I hate your guts," but global comments seldom yield significant results. Affirming someone's character or abilities is a skill that requires preparation and practice. It's easy, especially for verbal communicators, to become lazy in their praise of people. Instead, they need to think carefully about the people they lead, and then notice, name, and nurture the characteristics they value. Instead of saying to a volunteer, "Man, you're terrific," it's much more meaningful for a leader to think about that person, the obstacles he has overcome, and how God is using him in specific ways—the more descriptive, the better. Then, in a private moment or in a meeting, the leader might say, "Sean, I've been watching you, and I'm really impressed with how you care for people. You consistently go out of your way. I saw you take extra time with Mrs. Adams when she couldn't get the answer she needed and she was getting frustrated. She really appreciated your help, and I want you to know that I appreciate you, too."

There's no magic formula for authentic affirmation. We can focus on a pattern of behavior or praise a single event we noticed. We might point out character qualities like compassion, courage, or persistence, or we can focus on skills of administration or leadership. The most important element of affirming someone is that she realizes we've been thinking about her, and our comments aren't "out of the blue." There's certainly nothing wrong with spontaneous praise for people we lead, but praise is even more powerful when they are convinced that we have been watching and admiring them for a while. If we say too much too often, people discount what we say, and if we don't say enough, they wonder what we really think about them. We need a balanced approach to words of affirmation: not too seldom, not too often, but just the right amount at the right time.

Mutual affirmation among team members is particularly powerful. I read a story about a math teacher who asked her students to list the names of everyone in the class on a piece of paper, and to write the nicest thing they could think of about each one of them. After the class was over, she gathered all the papers. That night, she compiled all the statements for each student, and she presented the lists to each of them the next day in class. In a few minutes, everyone in the class was smiling. "Really?" one of them whispered to himself. "I didn't know I meant that much to anybody!" After that day, they never talked about the papers again.

> Mutual affirmation among team members is particularly powerful.

Several years later, one of the students was killed in Vietnam. His body was brought back to his hometown, and the teacher attended the funeral. As she filed by the casket with the other mourners, a soldier serving as a pallbearer asked her, "Were you Mark's math teacher?" She nodded, and he replied, "Mark talked about you a lot."

At a luncheon after the funeral, Mark's mother and father came over to speak to the teacher. His father said, "We want to show you something." He took a carefully folded piece of paper out of a wallet, and then he told her, "They found this on Mark when he was killed. We thought you might recognize it." Instantly, she saw that it was the list of statements Mark's classmates had written about him. His mother commented, "Thank you so much for doing that. As you can see, Mark treasured it." As they spoke, several other former students gathered around. One of them smiled and said, "I still have my list, too. It's in the top drawer of my desk at home." Others said they kept their list in a wedding album, in a diary, or in a purse. One of them spoke for the rest: "I think we all saved our lists." This dear teacher had invited students to affirm each other, and her simple assignment meant more to them than any subject they ever studied.

A Closer Look

How can we tell if our vocabulary is defining the culture we desire? We can pay attention to the signals we receive from the people around us, especially those closest to us. When their signals confuse us, we need to give ourselves permission to ask questions like, "What's going on? The people out there respond very well to my leadership, but those close to me look frustrated. Maybe I need to take a look at my words, my non-verbals, my congruence, and my authenticity." Feeling confused about our leadership isn't a bad thing. It's often the first step toward deeper analysis and change.

Good leaders regularly look at the culture of their teams and make necessary adjustments. They use asides to shine a light on the process of how the team relates to each other, and they inject affirmation, hope, and humor into the group at appropriate times. The discourse of a team tends to devolve to the lowest common denominator. If the range of people is from a Ph.D. to a high school graduate, the conversation tends to drift toward high school topics and a high school level of clarity. We need to be aware of that tendency so that we can intentionally direct the conversation to the middle level of the group. Then more people will stay engaged, and more will offer valuable input.

Changing culture always creates conflict. When we choose respect instead of manipulation, and honesty instead of avoidance of issues, most people will thrive, but a few resist even healthy changes. Don't be surprised when people on your team feel uncomfortable with honesty. Give them time to adjust, and keep loving them as you model a new vocabulary, but realize that some people may not want to participate in the new culture. They felt comfortable, and perhaps powerful, in the old one, and they prefer things to stay the way they were.

> Changing culture always creates conflict.

Our vocabulary, and especially the tone we use when we speak, powerfully defines and reflects culture. It's very easy to keep saying the same things in the same way over and over again, and expect different results—but that's a definition of insanity, not leadership. Unexamined vocabulary puts a ceiling on leadership.

Think About It . . .

1. What are some positive elements of your church's existing vocabulary? Which terms have you been using that hinder you from fulfilling God's vision?

2. Give an example of when you could use an aside with your team. How would you do it? What impact do you think it would have?

3. What are two specific principles or ideas from this chapter that you want to apply? How will you implement them?

5

CHANGE STARTS WITH ME

*It's amazing how someone's IQ seems to double as soon as
you give them responsibility and indicate that you trust them.*
—*Timothy Ferriss*

Phillip heard me speak at a conference, and during a break, he asked if I had time to meet with him. The next morning over coffee, he poured out his frustrations. He told me that he was on the executive team of a church of three thousand. "From your description of cultures," he informed me, "I'd say our church's culture is stagnant." I asked him to explain, and he told me that his senior pastor is a wonderful man and a good teacher, but Phillip has concluded that he has some serious flaws in his leadership. "We seem to be drifting. We have a vision statement, of course, but we don't seem to be focusing our energies and resources very well to achieve the vision." As we talked, I realized that Phillip's chief concerns were in the area of leadership development.

I probed a bit: "Tell me, what was your previous experience on a church staff?"

His eyes rolled and he shook his head, then said gravely, "It was a disaster. From your description, I'd say it was genuinely toxic."

"And you hoped this pastor, this staff, and this church would be different."

Phillip's eyes lit up. "Exactly. And for the first couple of years, it seemed like a dream come true. The problems have surfaced more recently."

"So Phillip," I continued to probe, "what would you like to do that the senior pastor won't let you do?"

He looked surprised. "Well, nothing. He's happy for me to do whatever I think God wants me to do."

"Oh really," I mused. "Tell me, then, what do you think is your biggest frustration?"

He looked at me as if he couldn't believe I didn't understand already, and then he almost shouted, "Dr. Chand, I want to serve on a team that is inspiring, where the whole team is on the same page, and together we're trusting God and working hard to achieve God's incredible, compelling, challenging purpose for us!"

Without batting an eye, I asked, "Do you have the freedom to create that kind of culture on your own team in your ministry area?"

Again, he looked surprised, and he said, "Well, yeah. I do." He paused to reflect for a few seconds, and then he told me, "I guess I should be grateful for that, huh?"

Some of us have exceptionally high expectations of the leaders and the organization where we serve. Unrealistically high expectations cloud our perspective, create unwarranted disappointment, and steal our emotional energy. Certainly, some cultures are so toxic that the best course is to leave as quickly and as graciously as possible, but far more often, the best place to start a revolution of change is in our own hearts and minds. Instead of waiting for the top leader to change the culture and make everything smooth, pleasant, and easy, we need to begin with the one person we have the power to control: ourselves.

One person can make a tremendous difference on a team, even if that person isn't the leader. When I became president of Beulah Heights University in 1989, the janitor was a man named Benson Karanja. On my last day in 2003, he became president of the university. How could someone make this kind of leap in leadership? At every level and in every role—from janitor to library assistant to librarian to administrator to professor to director of student affairs to vice president to executive VP and finally to president—he always gladly accepted responsibility and never deflected blame for wrong decisions on anyone else. As he assumed more leadership, he was always willing to ask the tough questions, but he asked in a way that didn't threaten anyone. Whenever any challenge needed to be analyzed, he said, "Dr. Chand, I'll examine this issue and give a report at our next meeting." Whenever a task needed to be done, he volunteered. His humble spirit convinced people that he wasn't jockeying for position. He was simply serving God and the university with every fiber of his being. And everyone around him felt challenged to give more, do more, and care more for God's kingdom. The janitor inspired a university.

> Unrealistically high expectations cloud our perspective, create unwarranted disappointment, and steal our emotional energy.

Replacing Disappointment

Christians, and especially those who serve in visionary churches, often have incredibly high expectations of their leaders. Like Phillip in the opening story in this chapter, they may have come from painful past situations in a family or church environment, and they hope, "This time, it'll be different!" They read glowing accounts of other churches, and they see how Jesus invited His followers to experience His love. They hope, pray, and expect—and too often demand—that this leader, this church,

> The number of "shoulds" in a person's mind and mouth is inversely proportional to his sense of peace, joy, and fulfillment.

and this team will be heaven on earth. (They need to read more of the New Testament to see how many problems most churches experienced, but that's a topic for another discussion.) Expectations surface in vocabulary. A word that appears in their conversations and thoughts is "should," as in, "The pastor should do this or that better," "He should lead this way or that way," "The board should give me more authority," and countless others. The number of "shoulds" in a person's mind and mouth is inversely proportional to his sense of peace, joy, and fulfillment.

To replace any nagging disappointment created by unrealistic expectations, let me suggest a few strategies:

+ Focus on what you can control.

+ Be tenaciously thankful.

+ Resolve any role alignment issues.

+ Invest creative capital.

Focus on What You Can Control

Many of us expend enormous amounts of energy worrying about and trying to manage things that are outside the realm of our control. To maintain mental and emotional health, and to be the kind of leaders and team members we can be, we have to realize that we aren't God. The scope of our responsibility and power is limited, and we need to devote our energies to those things that are inside our sandboxes. Thousands of recovery groups around the country use a German pastor and theologian's prayer to reframe their expectations. Most of us can quote the first part of Reinhold Niebuhr's "Serenity Prayer":

God grant me the serenity to accept the things I cannot change; courage to change the things I can; and wisdom to know the difference.

The rest of the prayer, though, gives even more insight about trusting God instead of ourselves:

Living one day at a time; Enjoying one moment at a time; Accepting hardships as the pathway to peace; Taking, as He did, this sinful world as it is, not as I would have it; Trusting that He will make all things right if I surrender to His Will; That I may be reasonably happy in this life and supremely happy with Him Forever in the next. Amen.

The first step, then, is for each of us to realize that we can't control the universe, or even the smaller universe of our church environment. For now, we need clear-eyed objectivity and optimism, with a commitment to do all we can to create a positive culture around us. Accepting responsibility for what we can control—and making a steadfast commitment not to complain about what's outside our control—are crucial ingredients in spiritual, emotional, and relational health.

> Accepting responsibility for what we can control—and making a steadfast commitment not to complain about what's outside our control—are crucial ingredients in spiritual, emotional, and relational health.

Be Tenaciously Thankful

Phillip had been missing out on much of the joy he could have been experiencing because his eyes had been riveted on the shortcomings of his senior pastor. It only took a few questions, though, for him to realize that God and his pastor had given him wonderful opportunities. His attitude almost immediately changed from griping to gratitude. From what I heard later, his thankful heart changed more than just his disposition. As the sludge of a critical spirit was washed away, he enjoyed his wife and family, his team, and every aspect of his ministry more than ever.

Resolve Any Role Alignment Issues

Sometimes a person's disappointment with a leader or a team runs deeper than attitude. When the job description doesn't fit the person's gifts and interests, confusion and heartache inevitably occur. The challenge of finding the best fit in a culture isn't always easy to resolve, but it's essential for each person to find, not the perfect fit, but a "good enough fit" so that the individual, the team, and the mission work well together.

Invest Creative Capital

In stagnant, discouraging, and toxic cultures, people spend their energies protecting themselves and creating alliances instead of creatively pursuing the mission. Even in accepting and inspiring cultures, individuals or pockets of people may live with deep disappointments caused by unrealistic expectations and shattered dreams. When people face these challenges with courage and hope, a new world opens up, and they can invest themselves in the cause that drew them there in the first place.

Characteristics of a Change Agent

Instead of waiting for the senior leaders or someone else to create a positive culture, each person on the team can take steps to be a change agent. Instead of waiting for someone to become trustworthy, each one can prove to be a trustworthy person; a man or woman of character, heart, and hope. There may be many different ways of describing people who, as leaders or team members, can shape organizational culture, but I want to offer my list of characteristics:

Heart motivation

Positive demeanor

Courage to ask tough questions

Honesty without limitations

Warmth and humor

Willingness to reflect reality

Heart Motivation

One of the first things to realize is that staff members and volunteers in the church world are motivated by meaning, not money. Dangling financial incentives to entice them to work harder proves to be counterproductive. They don't want to perceive that they are being treated unfairly in regard to salaries, but to touch their deepest motivations, leaders need to appeal to their desire for their lives to count.

Positive Demeanor

When the senior pastor says, "I believe God is calling us to trust him to pursue this vision," the atmosphere in the room is transformed if someone responds, "Pastor, we can trust God for that. Let's go for it." But a "can-do" spirit will only look like kissing up to the boss if another trait is missing…

Courage to Ask Tough Questions

Change agents need to be positive, but they need to be multidimensional: they must also possess the ability to ask penetrating questions to help the group discern God's will, to find the best alignment of roles and goals, and to develop the best plan for any challenge. In Benson Karanja, this rare and special combination of traits showed people that he was wise, humble, and optimistic. And as people spent more time around him, his attitude permeated every team on which he served.

Honesty About Limitations

People who claim to be able to do everything well lose the trust of those around them. Change agents are unfailingly optimistic, but they

> Being honest about holes in our skill set shows people that we aren't power hungry or driven to win approval.

also have a good grasp of their strengths and limitations. They are willing to say, "I can't do that very well, but I know someone who can." Being honest about holes in our skill set shows people that we aren't power hungry or driven to win approval. We notice others' strengths and affirm their contributions, and we gladly defer to them when they can do a job better than we can. In this way, everybody on the team feels valued.

Warmth and Humor

Every team needs someone who brings warmth to the relationships and can break the tension with humor from time to time. Remembering a birthday, a health concern, a child's struggle, or a joy in someone's life shows that we care about the people, not just the task they perform. Above all else, people want to know that others value them, and a word of warmth means everything to a team. And warmth is infectious. Just as one person's sour disposition can poison a team, an individual's sincere love for others can change the complexion of a meeting and a team.

Willingness to Reflect Reality

Unhealthy teams never talk about "the elephant in the room." They dance around uncomfortable topics, even though avoiding them further erodes trust among the people on the team. At that point, the refusal to talk about the issues is a bigger deal than the issues themselves. People who are cultural change agents are willing to say, "This is what I see going on with this issue," and even, "This is what I see going on with our team right now." Too often, leaders verbalize their perceptions only when they are so exasperated that they explode with their observations. That's not helpful. The first few times a leader practices healthy reflection, people on the team may feel uncomfortable simply because it's so novel. After a few times, though, team members realize that talking about "the process of processing" is essential to a healthy team culture.

> Talking about "the process of processing" is essential to a healthy team culture.

Practical Steps

For those of us who are serving in inspiring or accepting cultures, we simply want to sustain and enhance the quality of our relationships. Those who experience stagnant, discouraging, or toxic cultures, however, have more work to do to discover the right path forward. They may have been blasted for disagreeing with a leader, ignored and marginalized when they didn't measure up to the leader's expectations, or perhaps, even worse, patronized by insincere affirmations. In difficult cultures, people need to think clearly, avoid overreacting, and take wise steps. Let me offer a few suggestions:

+ Go to the leader privately.

+ Practice self-reflection.

+ Make a commitment.

+ Understand your equity and your risk tolerance.

+ If you leave, go gracefully.

Go to the Leader Privately

Never ever confront a senior leader publicly. It's a lose-lose-lose proposition. The leader gets angry because she loses face, you lose respect (and perhaps your job), and the culture goes backward because of escalating tension. One of the greatest needs in churches today is someone who can offer the light of perception to leaders. No one likes to be told, "You're a bad leader" or "You're not doing that the right way." But most leaders will listen if a team member approaches them privately and with grace and wisdom, saying "I've been thinking about this, and I want to tell you my observations." After sharing her thoughts, she doesn't demand a response. Instead, she tells the leader, "You don't need to tell me what you think about that. I just wanted you to know."

On a team, a person may have noticed that the team isn't communicating honestly and respectfully with each other. In that case, the person might go to the leader and say, "I've noticed that our team seems to have some tension, and I think it's preventing us from accomplishing all we could do together. I'm guessing that if I notice it, others sense it, too. I'm not asking you to fix it, and I'm not complaining. I just wanted to share my observation. Thanks for listening." Simply surfacing the issue brings it to the leader's attention without demanding a particular reply or action plan to correct it.

If the issue is the team's communication, a team member may assume that the problem is his own when he talks to the leader. He may say, "In the past few months, I've noticed that I seem to be holding back in the meeting each week. I'm not sure what's going on with me, but I was hoping you could help me figure it out. What do you think might be happening?"

A friend told me that he used to experience significant tension in his relationship with his senior pastor. As the tension mounted, he planned more carefully how he would handle every conversation, but the problem only got worse. When he talked to a wise friend, the friend told him, "You're coming across as defiant and demanding. Instead, start each conversation with this phrase, 'Pastor, I need your help.' That will put him at ease and make him an ally instead of an adversary." My friend started using that technique, and he said it turned their relationship around 180 degrees.

> It's far healthier for everybody if each team member accepts responsibility for his own behavior and learns to communicate respectfully and wisely with the leader and the rest of the team.

The title of this chapter is "Change Starts with Me." We don't want to communicate with a leader in a tone and using words that demand that he or she change—or else! When we come across in a condescending or demanding tone, we are hoping that change will start (and end) with the leader. It's far healthier for everybody if each team member accepts responsibility for his own behavior and learns to communicate respectfully and wisely with the leader and the rest of the team.

Practice Self-Reflection

Wise people notice dissonance in their emotions, thoughts, and relationships, and they take time to ask themselves, *What's that about?* As reflection becomes the habit of a lifetime, they are less surprised when they uncover selfish motives and harmful behaviors that may have been part of their lives since they were children.

Self-reflection is both planned and spontaneous. A question that I teach people to ask about themselves at regular intervals is, "What is it about *me* that keeps *me* from becoming the best *me* that God intended *me* to be?" This question invites us to take full responsibility for

> "What is it about me that keeps me from becoming the best me that God intended me to be?"

our growth and direction, and it rivets our purpose to God's plan for our lives. I'd encourage leaders and team members to take time to reflect on this question three or four times a year. But through the years, I've also learned to pay attention to little flashes of confusion, which are the first signs of insight. When I'm talking with someone and I say something that sounds odd, I may reflect, *I wonder why I said that.* Or as I'm preparing a message and working on a particular point that I've made hundreds of times in the past, I may feel some emotional disturbance and ask myself, *Why would I say it that way? There seems to be a demand in those words. What's that about?* Or if I find myself in a situation that used to bother me but doesn't any longer, I wonder, *What's changed? Is it a good thing or a bad thing that it doesn't bother me anymore?*

For leaders and team members, confusion about their hearts and their roles isn't the biggest problem they face. I believe the dissonance that comes from being responsive to the Spirit's prompting may be unsettling for a while, but it opens a door to insight, growth, and better connections with the people we love.

All of us need honest feedback from a spouse and close friends, but we need to be careful that we are asking for the truth, not lobbying for allies to defend us. Try approaching a few very close friends and asking, "Do you see any patterns that have surfaced lately in my attitudes and actions with the staff team? I think I've turned into a jerk. I've responded with anger over even little things. Have you seen that in me?" And they'll tell you what they've seen.

Make a Commitment

Make a solemn commitment to be the best team member or leader you can be. Reflect on the attitude that has shaped your response, your skills in engaging your leader, and the impact you're having on others—and be honest with what you find. Think carefully about how to display the characteristics of a change agent, and take the risk to speak up, ask questions, offer encouragement, and be the kind of trustworthy person you want others to be.

If you're discouraged about your leader, step back and consider the pressures he's under. Leading people is very difficult, and even the best leaders aren't always successful. Just look at Jesus! Your leader may have suffered some losses that you haven't considered, or there may be family struggles, financial needs, health concerns, or other difficulties that rob him of stability.

> Be the kind of leader you want others to be.

Make a commitment to lead your own team with integrity, love, and skill. Be the kind of leader you want others to be. Even if you feel like a Lone Ranger, lead with passion and grace. As you lead your team, don't criticize your pastor or any other leaders in the church. And if your team members begin speaking negatively, stop them and explain how gossip ruins attitudes and relationships. God has a purpose for you as you lead your team. Look for Him to lead you in every interaction with those you lead and with those on the team on which you serve as a member.

Understand Your Equity and Your Risk Tolerance

I've watched some staff members become angry or righteously indignant (depending on who's telling the story) and leave their position without thought of the implications to their families. I'm not advocating that anyone stay in a toxic, abusive environment one day longer than necessary, but you need to be aware of the consequences and timing of your choices.

To understand the context of your decision more fully, consider these questions:

+ "Could I have misunderstood my leader?"

I've known spouses who have misinterpreted each other's behavior for many years, so it's certainly possible that you could have misunderstood the leader's words, actions, and especially motives.

+ "How long has the problem been going on?"

If the difficulty with the leader has occurred only in the past few weeks, you need to be more patient and see if the problem vanishes as quickly as it appeared. Look for established patterns. Don't be too concerned about isolated blips on the radar. Of course, if the problem is sexual harassment or another form of blatant disrespect, you don't need any additional time to look for patterns. The severity and nature of the issue determine how patient you should be in trying to resolve it, cope with it, or confront it.

+ "Am I oversensitive about defending my role or my department?"

Is the issue you are so upset about systemwide, or is it possible that a decision is being made for the good of the whole that seems unfair or inconsiderate to your department? Sometimes leaders make global decisions, but they don't explain them so that each department leader understands why the choice was made.

+ "Do I have anywhere to go?"

It's not appropriate to use office hours to look for a position at a different church, unless of course you have permission from your team leader or pastor. I've seen men and women resign "on principle" with nowhere to go. If they had waited a little longer, they may have been able to make an exit more gracefully for everyone involved.

+ "How does my decision affect my family?"

Decisions to resign in the heat of the moment seldom consider a spouse's employment or children's school situations. Consider the broader implications of the decision, not just how it makes you feel in your role and work relationships.

If You Leave, Go Gracefully

At some point, some of us will come to the conclusion that we can't be effective in the culture where we serve, and it's time to leave. If we have learned to live and serve with integrity and wisdom in a difficult culture, we will experience deep sadness for our own loss and for those who remain, because we care for them. However, if we haven't learned the lessons of being change agents, we'll either explode in anger or slink away in shame (or perhaps a combination of those painful emotions).

A young man came up to me at a conference and told me, "Dr. Chand, my name is Jackson. I love being a youth pastor, and I'm thrilled to see God work in students' lives, but the struggle to serve at our church is killing me. The drama on our staff team is killing me. It's ridiculous. Everything is a huge hassle. I've tried to make it work. I've tried to do all the things you teach about having a great attitude, affirming others, approaching my senior pastor with wisdom...all of that, but it's just not working. I go home each night emotionally exhausted. When I think about the student ministry, I can't wait to get up and get going each day, but then I think of the relationships on our staff team, and I want to run away. What should I do?"

I counseled Jackson to go back and give it one more shot, to talk with his pastor and try to find a way for it to work. I explained that he needed to know it was God's direction for him to leave or stay. It wasn't good enough to "go with his gut." I asked him to call me in a few months to let me know how it was going. Several months later, Jackson telephoned and told me, "Dr. Chand, I gave it my best shot, and I'm completely convinced that God wants me to leave. How can I do it gracefully?"

I gave Jackson a brief set of directions for a graceful exit:

+ Meet with the pastor and thank him for the opportunity to serve at the church. Explain that you believe God is leading you to serve at another church. Tell him that you want to make the transition to the next person as smooth as possible. Ask him what he wants you to do to make that happen (for example, related to teams, contact Information with students, schedules, commitments for camps, and so on).

+ When the pastor or others ask why you are leaving (and they will), don't use the moment as an opportunity to "clear the air" and blast the pastor and other leaders. Keep it pleasant, thankful, and future centered.

+ The hardest conversations are often with the top volunteers, many of whom know the struggles and have great compassion for the person leaving. Don't let these conversations devolve into angry blaming sessions. Thank people for their hearts and their service, and celebrate all the things God has done through you as you served together.

> We don't all have to be the same for the body to work well, but we have to be committed to a common purpose—loving one another in spite of our differences and resolving disagreements agreeably.

◆ Pave the way for the new person by leaving everything in great shape.

We need to remember that God calls His church to unity, not uniformity. We don't all have to be the same for the body to work well, but we have to be committed to a common purpose—loving one another in spite of our differences and resolving disagreements agreeably.

The Process of Change

Most organizational consultants report that it takes about three years to change the culture of a team, a church, a nonprofit organization, or a business. I've seen this process as occurring in four stages, illustrated by this diagram:

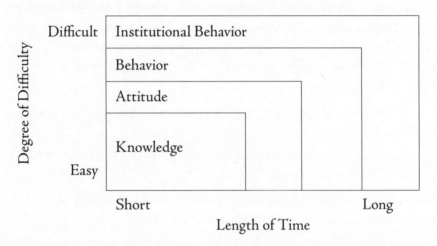

Originally developed by Sam Williams and adapted by Carol Childress, cited in "Levels of Change, Part 2," Leadership Network Champions Fax, Volume 3 Number 2, January 26, 1998.

Knowledge

The first level requires a change of mind resulting in increased knowledge. Facts that support the reasons for change need to be gathered and shared. Facts are far more persuasive than opinions, but facts alone don't produce culture change. In fact, they can precipitate conflict because everyone may not agree on what needs to be done or be ready to do it.

We gain knowledge by reading books and articles, attending seminars, and listening to friends who are learning important lessons about taking responsibility for their roles in the cultures of their churches or teams.

Attitude

The second level requires a change in attitudes about roles, goals, and relationships. In this stage, people may feel threatened because their rituals, expectations, and job descriptions are being examined. Quite often, leaders react by producing more information to support their views, but this is counterproductive. The issue now is emotional, not intellectual, and the leader's role is to provide support, listen carefully, and help people steer through the emotional minefields that always accompany culture change.

> The leader's role is to provide support, listen carefully, and help people steer through the emotional minefields that always accompany culture change.

At this level, our knowledge seeps into our hearts and produces convictions. We determine, "I don't want to act that way with Barbara anymore. I want to be kind and affirming, not short with her." As a team talks about the culture and its implications, don't be surprised when people become defensive. Turf issues surface very quickly at this point, but patiently listen. Let fears run their course. Answer questions, reassure people of their importance and their roles, and look to the future.

Behavior

The third level requires a change in behavior, and as those behaviors become habits, a new lifestyle becomes the norm in the culture. Each change may begin with incremental choices that feel relatively safe and offer the biggest chance for success. As those new behaviors come to feel natural, the leader and the team can move to the next, and perhaps more challenging, priority.

We may apply the principles of becoming a change agent in different ways, but all of us will take action in this level. Some of us instinctively remember a concern shared by someone in the last meeting, so we ask about it as the next meeting begins, but some of us need to write down those concerns to remind us to ask about them. If we realize that we talk to a particular team member only at the meetings, we may want to go to that person's office a few minutes before the next meeting to say something like, "Kim, I really appreciate the wisdom you share in our meetings. I wish we had more time together. I could learn a lot from you. Thanks for your contribution to the team."

We have different talents, different backgrounds, and different experiences, but everyone on the team plays an important role in shaping the culture of the team. During this stage of culture change, each person realizes his or her unique contribution, spoken by the person and affirmed by the team. The team leader may lead the culture, but it is sustained and deepened by the team members.

> The team leader may lead the culture, but it is sustained and deepened by the team members.

Institutional Behavior

The fourth level, which is the cumulative effect of knowledge, attitudes, and new habits, requires a change in the culture of the organization. Each person on the team has had time to think, plan, and experiment with new actions that, over time, take root and change the expectations and relationships.

Happiness and Effectiveness

In their thoughts and expectations, most people instinctively link happiness and effectiveness. They assume that the two are always mutually inclusive, but in observing people in hundreds of organizations, I can report that this isn't necessarily true. I've talked to people in stagnant and discouraging cultures, and even a few in toxic environments, who found a way to be effective in their work. They endured their team's passivity or pathology by putting their heads down and being the best they could be at the work God had given them to do. They weren't particularly happy, but they found a measure of satisfaction in "working heartily, as unto the Lord," and seeing lives changed. By contrast, I've not known anyone who was ineffective at the task she was commissioned to perform but found genuine joy on a team. God has made us so that we thrive emotionally at work only when we know we are contributing our knowledge and skills to accomplish something bigger than ourselves. Those who spend their lives complaining and dodging responsibility find neither happiness nor effectiveness.

> We thrive emotionally at work only when we know we are contributing our knowledge and skills to accomplish something bigger than ourselves.

Self-Analysis

To discover the kind of impact we're having on our teams, let me offer a few topics for self-analysis:

- Analyzing current relationships
- Clarifying expectations
- Living with ambiguity
- Gleaning the wisdom of new voices
- Monitoring deposits and withdrawals

Analyzing Current Relationships

When we examine our roles and our effectiveness, our first questions need to focus on relationships, not organizational issues or role competency. Our ability to connect with people, earn their trust, invite their opinions, and inspire them is the most important trait we bring—even more important than our experiences or skills. When we experience stress, we need to ask, "What patterns have shifted in my family, in my relationships with friends, and in my relationships with people on my team?" Quite often, significant shifts in key relationships show up as job stress. We internalize a deep sense of loss or the threat of loss, and we become defensive, demanding, or withdrawn. It's easy to see that what happens in the office affects how we relate to our spouse and children, but the reverse is also true: shifts in patterns of relationships at home can have a dramatic impact on relationships at work. Emotional health is primarily a function of relationships, not competence in our roles.

Clarifying Expectations

Idealism may be a good beginning, but it seldom serves leaders and team members well as they try to form a healthy atmosphere. "Shoulds" need to be replaced by an unvarnished grasp of reality—not at the expense of hope, but with the hope-filled expectation that God will use flawed people in often messy processes to accomplish His divine purposes. People who cling to idealism inevitably become disappointed and discouraged.

Living with Ambiguity

All of us need to gain the skill of living in ambiguity, knowing that we live between the *already* of God's fulfilled promises and the *not yet* of those that will be fulfilled only when we see Him face-to-face. High-impact leaders and team members are like a car with three gears: forward, reverse, and neutral.

> Outstanding leaders and team members don't feel pressured to make instant decisions.

People with only two gears, forward and reverse, have little capacity for careful reflection. They feel uncomfortable with ambiguity and the tension of waiting. Outstanding leaders and team members, however, don't feel pressured to make instant decisions. They can listen carefully tocompeting interests, ask penetrating questions, invite more dialogue, and say, "I don't know" until the answer eventually surfaces. Staying in neutral for a while enables them to listen, gain more insight, reflect, involve people, and gain God's wisdom on difficult matters.

Gleaning the Wisdom of New Voices

All of us need the challenge and the stimulation of hearing new concepts from new voices, but we need to be careful that we don't let those new voices poison our perspective. For example, a friend of mine listened to podcasts of a brilliant pastor teaching a doctoral course. He instinctively compared the pastor-prof to the pastor at his church, and his pastor suddenly dropped a few notches on his respect grid. One of the marks of a healthy person and a good team member is that we're always learning, absorbing new concepts and testing new strategies. But the urge to compare is often a tragic trait of human nature. If we're not careful, we'll use the new voices as a club to condemn others who don't measure up to our new standards. With a warning against graceless comparison, we need to ask ourselves,

+ Who are the new voices that have recently inspired me?

+ What are some books that have challenged my thinking in the past few weeks?

+ What concepts, strategies, or visions have produced in me a sense of godly discontent?

These questions focus more on *being* than *doing*, more on the ontology of who we are than on what function we perform. Too often, we focus our development strategies on roles and skills instead of heart and character, but trust is primarily a response to the internal rather than the external characteristics of a person. God created Adam and Eve as perfect human beings, but after they sinned, the curse gave them arduous tasks to do. And still today, we define ourselves and describe each other by the things we do instead of by heart and character. In the Garden, mankind shifted from acceptance, grace, and love to blame, shame, and the compulsion to prove ourselves by our performance. To recapture God's design, we need new voices that penetrate our crusty defenses and speak to our souls, not only inspiring our actions but, even more, inflaming our hearts.

Monitoring Deposits and Withdrawals

There are two types of people in our lives, those who make deposits and those who make withdrawals. We can't orchestrate our lives to eliminate interactions with people who take more than they give to us, but if we are wise, we will do two crucial things: we'll limit our time with the takers, and we'll make sure we spend time with the ones who add to our emotional bank accounts. As we comprehend this principle, we'll be more understanding and patient with senior leaders. If we spent time with them each day, we'd see that 99 percent of their interactions are with people who make withdrawals. Almost every phone call they receive is someone saying, "Pastor, I need this," or "Pastor, I'm upset about that." When that pastor is less than perfectly gracious in a meeting, we might conclude that he has endured too many withdrawals and too few deposits lately. An accurate perception of the effect of givers and takers in his life encourages us to be compassionate instead of judgmental.

> There are two types of people in our lives, those who make deposits and those who make withdrawals.

In stagnant, discouraging, and toxic cultures, people form alliances to provide self-protection and self-validation. The people involved might claim that these interactions are important deposits in their lives, especially compared to the passivity or abuse they experience in relationships with others in the culture. But people in these alliances need to take a long, hard look at the impact of these conversations. Do they bring truth, honor, and life, or do they perpetuate resentment and gossip? In negative cultures, even "supportive" relationships make withdrawals disguised as deposits.

The commitment of each of us is to be the best team member we can be and, on our own teams, to create an inspiring culture. When we look at the culture of any organization, we don't look only at the top leaders. It is the leaders' responsibility to shape the values and the environment, but culture percolates from every nook and cranny of the organization. As we've noted earlier, a toxic environment is like carbon monoxide; you can't see it, but it'll kill you. And an inspiring culture is like perfume, filling the air with the sweet aroma of love, encouragement, passion, and a commitment to excellence.

Perhaps the most important principle in this chapter is that each person is responsible for shaping the culture. It's not acceptable to sit back and complain about how we've been mistreated or how clueless our leaders are. Remaining passive and resentful, or being demanding and furious, certainly creates a culture, but not a good one. On the spectrum of smells, we can all make the commitment to bring an aroma of life instead of carrying around the smell of cultural death.

Think About It . . .

4. How can a person have a thankful, positive attitude no matter how difficult the culture may be?

5. Look at the characteristics of a change agent. On a scale of 0 (not at all) to 10 (exceptionally well), give yourself a grade on how you're doing with each one right now.

   ____ Heart motivation

   ____ Positive demeanor

   ____ Ability to ask tough questions

   ____ Honesty about limitations

   ____ Warmth and humor

_____ Willingness to reflect reality

6. Write down the names of people with whom you have your most important relationships at home, socially, and at work. Next to each one write "deposit" if that person's net impact on you fills you with encouragement, hope, and love, and write "withdrawal" next to those whose net impact drains you. Finally, reflect on the pattern of deposits and withdrawals in your life and complete this sentence:

   No wonder I feel . . .

7. Look at the list again, and for each person answer this question: In her relationship with you, would she say you are making a net deposit or a withdrawal in her life? When you are finished marking "deposit" or "withdrawal" for each one, consider this question: What needs to happen for you to make deposits in more people's lives?

8. What are some specific steps you can take today or in your next meeting to be the best team member you can be and to lead your team in creating an inspiring culture?

6

THE CATALYST OF CHAOS

If you have a job without aggravations, you don't have a job.
—*Malcolm Forbes*

To create a new culture, you have to destroy the old one. Half measures won't do. If we try to ease our way into a new culture with as little pain as possible, we'll probably fail to make the necessary adjustments, and any change we make will be incomplete or nonexistent. Expect blood on the floor. To galvanize people's resolve to kill the old and raise up a new culture, every growing organization has to make friends with an odd ally: chaos. The commitment to change a culture is always learned from negative experiences that look like chaos but are actually open doors to a new world of creativity and growth. These experiences often take the form of failure, conflict, and power struggles, but chaos also is the result of implementing bold new plans when other

> To create a new culture, you have to destroy the old one.

people want to rest on past success. In the crucible of chaos, God forms our character, creates a new culture, and determines our destiny.

Stakes in the Ground

All organizations experience change. Even churches that treasure their ancient traditions have to find ways to connect with people in a high-speed, postmodern world. Some people feel threatened by the speed of change even more than by the actual changes, and some resist change because they feel uncomfortable during the awkward time of uncertainty between the old normal and the new normal. The pace of change in our society is so fast today that leaders in every field desperately try to find ways to keep up. Most leaders try to anticipate the changes that will occur in the next five to ten years. (Who would have dreamed that the technology that gave us "mobile phones" we carried like suitcases twenty years ago would produce the Internet connected smart phones we use today? And what will we use twenty years from now?) But Jeff Bezos, founder and president of Amazon.com, has a different perspective. He focuses on the things that will remain the same "because you can really spin up flywheels around those things," he observes. "All the energy you invest in them today will still be paying dividends 10 years from now." This perspective encourages leaders and their teams to value a few things that won't change, but it has the positive result of putting everything else on the table for evaluation and change. What does Bezos say won't change? In his world, it's selection, low prices, and fast delivery.[1]

In the church world, many things have changed since the Ascension, but we can count on a few constants: God's Word is the source of truth, His Spirit changes lives, people value authentic leadership, and they thrive in close-knit communities of faith. These things are the stakes in the ground we can always count on. Many people who feel threatened by change are secretly (and perhaps unconsciously) wondering if their bedrock values are going to be thrown out along with the changes to worship songs, choir robes, small group content, and service times. If they are convinced that the church's core values will always be respected, they may be more willing to embrace changes in other areas.

All cultures are shifting, but thankfully, not everything in those cultures is changing, or we'd suffer from an overload of dislocation. In our family, Brenda and I still live in the same house we've enjoyed for many years, she teaches at the same school, and I do the same work with the same kind of pastors, but even in our stable world, we experience pleasant surprises, unanticipated challenges, nagging difficulties, and wonderful new opportunities. All of these demand our attention and call for us to change.

As we examine chaos as the catalyst of change, we need to remember that our people have varying capacities to embrace change. Some are terrified by it, and a few thrive in it, but they all ask a fundamental question at every step: "How does it affect me?" The way a leader navigates change may do more to define the organization's culture than any purpose state-

> The way a leader navigates change may do more to define the organization's culture than any purpose statement.

ment. The path charted through threats and opportunities demonstrates the actual values of the leader, the team, and the organization. The response to chaos, then, is both a reflection of the existing culture and an open door to cultural change.

I've seen leaders experience chaos in countless ways, but three of those ways stand out as unique challenges: redefining failure, creating a sense of urgency to take advantage of opportunities, and managing conflict. Let's look at each of these.

Redefining Failure

Today, innovation is a key component of growing churches, but fresh approaches carry an inherently higher risk of failure than safer paths.

Truly innovative leaders and their teams not only encourage people to dream new ideas and find new solutions but also have found a way to transform the inevitable failures into platforms for future success. They recognize the nature of risk and are realistic about the possibility—and even the probability—of failure. They know that Magellan hit scores of dead ends before he found the passage around the tip of South America to the Pacific, Edison experimented with hundreds of materials before he found the carbon filament for the light bulb, medical researchers work for years to find a single drug to fight a disease, and many authors are turned down by dozens of publishers before they find one who will put their work in print. If these men and women had quit after the first (or fiftieth) failure, the world wouldn't have the benefit of their discoveries and insights. In a similar way, Christians need to ask,

What are we willing to risk for God's kingdom?

What is the point when we give up hope and quit trying to implement change?

How do we treat others when they fail?

I encourage pastors to create a culture of experimentation in which creativity is celebrated and failure isn't a tragedy. By its nature, innovation breeds a form of chaos because each day people say to themselves and each other, "I wonder if this will work." In these environments, we see versions of the "happy warrior," but here it's the "happy innovator" who is willing to risk his time, money, and reputation to see if God might bless a new way of doing things. Of course, creativity has to be guided by wisdom, but excessive caution shouldn't rule our lives. There are always far more people who say, "Don't" or "Wait" than those who eagerly say, "Let's go for it!"

> I encourage pastors to create a culture of experimentation in which creativity is celebrated and failure isn't a tragedy.

Pastors and team leaders certainly don't enjoy falling on their faces, but instead of spending their emotional capital pointing fingers and defending themselves, they can develop a culture that redefines failure and replaces condemnation with tenacious hope. To create this kind of culture, leaders need to apply a few simple but important principles:

+ Look in the mirror to see how you respond to failure.

+ Develop a vocabulary of risk.

+ Respond positively to success.

+ Respond graciously to failure.

Look in the Mirror to See How You Respond to Failure

Some of us try to be positive when others fail, but we harshly condemn ourselves for our own failures. It's very difficult to offer patience, hope, and wisdom to others when we don't experience it personally. We have to draw water from a full (or at least a filling) well.

Develop a Vocabulary of Risk

People long to follow a leader who blends vision and wisdom, but they soon become skeptical of a wild-eyed visionary or, on the other end of the spectrum, a leader who is too cautious to take any risks at all. Think about the leaders you admire, the ones who are thoughtful, caring, and willing to attempt great things for God. How do they communicate at every level: with their top leaders, all their staff, the church, and the community? What kinds of words and phrases do they use? What are the nonverbal signals they send to those who are watching and listening? The goal isn't to take wild and crazy risks but to bring people along to trust God to accomplish His purposes—and His purposes are always big enough to enflame the hearts of His people.

Respond Positively to Success

The way leaders respond to success is a predictor of how they'll respond to failure. A healthy culture celebrates success, but it always

A healthy culture celebrates success.

takes time to reflect on what went right and what could be better next time. And it's important to give credit where credit is due: to the Lord and to the hard work of men and women who trusted God to use them. Leaders who take too much credit for themselves erode trust, discourage followers, and drip toxins into the culture.

Some leaders have exceptionally high expectations of success, and they are devastated by anything less. I knew a pastor whose standard for success was that his church would grow by 18 percent each year. When it grew at that rate or higher, he walked into meetings with confidence and joy, full of emotional deposits to share with others. But when his church grew only 16 percent one year, he saw it as a personal failure and a failure of his staff. He grumbled to express his displeasure, and he thought about firing several staff members. Instead of making deposits in others' lives, he took out hefty withdrawals. Couldn't he celebrate 16 percent growth? Apparently not.

Success means different things to different people at different times in their lives. To this pastor, the measure of success was the rate of growth—in fact, a consistently high rate of growth of his church. At one point, success for me was determined by how much money I made. Today, I measure it by how much impact God gives me in the lives of leaders. Bob Buford, the founder of Leadership Network, has written eloquently about the need to shift our attention from success to significance. I believe there is a category after that: fulfillment, the sweet spot at the intersection of God's gifting in our lives, people's needs, and our joy at seeing lives changed.

Respond Graciously to Failure

Many people come from families and church cultures where failure was condemned in one way or another. There may not have been name-calling and raised voices, but the one responsible got "that look" that spoke a thousand words of blame and disappointment. Attempting great things for God always results in a mixed bag of success and failure. Expect it, and don't come unglued when failure happens. Look people in the eye, reassure them with an affirmation that they went for it with boldness and faith, and make a point of asking two forward-looking questions:

1. What did you learn?

2. What will you do next time?

Ironically, some Christians feel particularly threatened by failure because they believe that God's involvement should guarantee success. They forget that responding to failure with faith is the cornerstone of the Christian life, and the examples in the scriptures are almost limitless. Peter denied Christ three times after proudly professing that he was willing to die for him, Paul lists many times when he faced brutal opposition to his efforts to tell people about Jesus, and it seemed to the whole world that Christ Himself had failed miserably when He died that Friday afternoon to the jeers of His enemies. But in all these cases, apparent failure became the launching pad for a demonstration of God's amazing work of grace and power. As sinners saved by grace, we face our own failures time after time, but we, too, find new opportunities to experience light in each moment of darkness.

Failure isn't the end of the world. In fact, if we develop an optimistic, forward-thinking culture of experimentation, failure can be the platform to learn life's greatest lessons so that we can continue to think the unimaginable, dream the impossible, and attempt incredible things for God. Redefining failure for your team and your church is a vital part of creating a strong, inspiring culture. Stop playing not to lose, and start playing to win.

> Failure can be the platform to learn life's greatest lessons so that we can continue to think the unimaginable, dream the impossible, and attempt incredible things for God.

Anticipate Opportunities

Every organization experiences natural cycles of growth and decline. British author Charles Handy has popularized the Sigmoid Curve to encourage leaders of change. The cycle begins with an energizing vision and moves into a growth mode. If momentum isn't sustained, energy gradually subsides, and passion erodes into empty regimentation and lifeless institutionalization. Finally, decline leads to stagnation and death. At that point, people remember the "good old days" when the vision was fresh and strong. In the diagram, point A marks the period when the vision begins to fade, but decline doesn't occur until later, at point B.

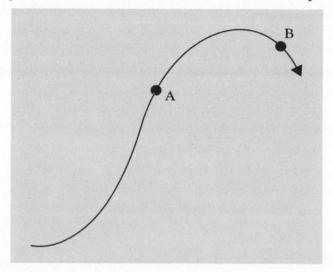

Vision, Growth, Decline, Stagnation, and Death

Churches may be at point A when a successful building campaign has been completed, a new small group emphasis has doubled the size of that ministry, a bold outreach has seen hundreds come to Christ and join the church, a new discipleship philosophy and strategy has profoundly shaped people's lives, or any other major emphasis in the church has been successful. At that moment, leaders and followers are tempted to take a deep breath and conclude, "Wow, that was great. Let's take a break for a while." They don't realize that the failure to capitalize on the momentum is the beginning point of decline. In fact, most leaders don't recognize the need for change until point B, when decline has already become a reality.

Great leaders have the foresight to predict the need at point A for a fresh vision and change, before decline sets in at point B. Communicating this perspective is a difficult task because very few people, if anyone, in the organization sees a need to "fix" what isn't broken. At this pivotal moment, visionary leaders need to infuse a successful system with a sense of urgency that change is necessary—right now before it's too late! But this attempt carries a risk. Communicating a fresh vision for change during a time of peace is seen by some as a power trip on the part of the leader. They question his motives—and perhaps his sanity. Great leaders, though,

> Great leaders are often misunderstood, especially when they create chaos when everyone expects a time of tranquility.

are often misunderstood, especially when they create chaos when everyone expects a time of tranquility.

If a leadership team takes action at point A and infuses the church with a new vision, strategy, and heart, they can change the shape of the curve and experience another growth cycle. The time between the envisioning of the new wave at point A and the upward movement after a period of preparation (often two or three years) is full of doubt, fear, and questions—a time of chaos.

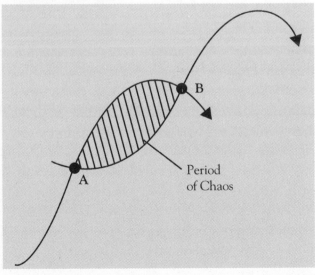

B

Period
of Chaos

A

When the leader makes the change at point A, he will inevitably incur misunderstanding from many and resistance from some. In the season of chaos between point A and point B, people are in a state of flux, routines have been disturbed, and the security of the familiar is absent. This chaos can certainly be avoided, but only if the leader waits until it's obvious the change is needed at point B. At this point, however, it's too late to stay on top of the game. We must change before the need to change is obvious. Constant growth means consistent chaos. Consequently, if an organization wants to continue to grow, the leaders must invite chaos to be their constant companion. At every recurring point A, they recognize the need for more change, a new vision—and chaos!

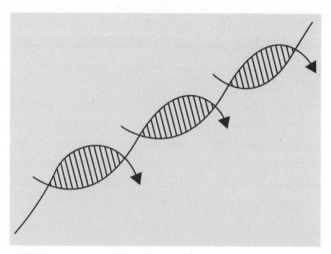

If the leader and the organization are secure enough to endure it, this chaotic, flexible mode of operation will provide a path to the future. The blunt truth is that all of us experience change. The question is this: Will we change too late? Church consultant Thomas G. Bandy looked into the hearts of leaders who anticipate opportunities and predicted, "The future of the church in the 21st century will not be determined by planning. It will be determined by leadership development. These leaders may be clergy or laity, and they will probably not care about the designation. They will be risk takers and adventurers. They will always be wondering what opportunity lies over the next cultural hill. They will be explorers of the unknown. They will be you."

The following are important diagnostic questions for leaders to consider:

Questions About Chaos

In the last ten to fifteen years, when were the times when your church experienced significant momentum?

What created the momentum?

How did you respond when you had momentum? Did you capitalize on it, or did you let it drift away?

When I spoke to a group of pastors to explain the importance of capturing momentum at point A, Rick came up to me at the next break. He blurted out, "Oh my gosh, Dr. Chand. I get it! I didn't get it until now, but now I get it."

I had no doubt he was going to share his story with me, but I asked anyway: "What is it that you now get?"

"When you talked about looking back to see how we responded when our church had momentum, I suddenly realized what happened. Three times in the past twelve years we experienced a tremendous surge of new people when God blessed us. We were clearly at point A."

"And how did you respond?" I asked.

"We blew it," Rick said with more joy for finding insight than sorrow for missing those opportunities. "We just blew it. Each time, we coasted. Oh, we were very thankful for God's blessings, and we worked hard to incorporate all those people into the life of the church, but within six months to a year, the momentum began to subside." His eyes widened with a fresh insight, and he told me, "And you know something? It's a lot easier to capture and build on existing momentum than to generate it from scratch."

We continued to talk, and he shared his current situation. His church was completing a new worship center. It was scheduled to open in five months, and they expected to grow by 30 percent in the first few weeks after the grand opening. Rick observed, "Dr. Chand, I've focused our staff on those first few months after we get into our new building. That's when we'll have incredible momentum. But I haven't even thought about how to capture that momentum and plan for the next three years. Today we're going to start our next phase of chaos!"

I kept up with Rick over the next few months. He went back from the pastors' conference and explained the concept of capturing momentum at point A to his senior staff and board. I asked him how those conversations went, and he told me, "Most of the people looked at me like they believed an alien had taken over their pastor's body. They couldn't imagine planning another big surge a few years down the road when we hadn't even gotten into our new building. But by the time the first meeting was over, a few of my staff realized the importance of taking advantage of the momentum God was going to give us. In a few weeks of many, many conversations and explanations, most of the others on our team finally came on board."

"Did you have any that simply refused to sign on to the vision God has given you?" I asked.

Rick smiled in a sad way and told me, "We have a couple of openings I'd like to fill."

"I understand," I nodded.

"Dr. Chand, I'm so excited about the future. I finally understand how we failed to capitalize on momentum in the past, and I don't plan to make that mistake ever again. I feel like I have a whole new way to think about our church and plan more strategically. Thank you so much for turning on the lights for me."

When leaders understand the importance of anticipating and implementing change at point A instead of waiting until decline happens at point B, they can infuse their culture with optimism and urgency. Award-winning author John Kotter observes, "Central to a continuous change culture is a continuously high sense of urgency. It does not follow a pattern of recognizing we have a problem, solving the problem, and going back to a sense of complacency. It's a culture that constantly reinforces the behaviors of being alert, of being curious, of doing it now, of leading no matter where you are in the organization."[2] Most leaders, Kotter asserts, think they are doing a great job of injecting urgency into their cultures, but a few conversations with people on their teams suggest otherwise. Organizations naturally drift toward complacency instead of urgency, fear rather than optimism, and blaming others instead of taking responsibility. To overcome this drift, leaders can invite fresh, challenging ideas to stimulate creative thinking, tell stories to capture people's hearts, and be models of urgency for their team members.

> When leaders understand the importance of anticipating and implementing change at point A instead of waiting until decline happens at point B, they can infuse their culture with optimism and urgency.

In his insightful book *The Incestuous Workplace*, William White observes that the sickest cultures are those that close their doors to new ideas. Closed organizations thrive on "rigid, unchallengeable organizational belief systems" and "progressive isolation" from the outside world. The absence of fresh thinking robs the organization of creativity and the stimulation of new ideas, and soon, people turn inward, creating institutional stagnation.[3] The options for opening the system to fresh ideas are almost endless. Leadership teams have used consultants, seminars, and books to challenge their thinking and their strategies. Some have invited people in the community to visit a staff meeting to share their impressions of the church. New hires can bring a fresh perspective to a team and shake up the old order in a healthy way. Almost anything can help if the leader invites new thinking to challenge the status quo. The goal isn't to throw everything out the window and start over every few months, but to be always open to new ideas and fresh ways of fulfilling the vision God has given the church. Teams that are open to new concepts continually ask, "What can we do better?" and "What can we learn from others?" These questions raise the intellectual antennae, heighten awareness, and infuse the team with enthusiasm.

Urgency rarely comes from graphs on a presentation. PowerPoint slides and charts on paper may communicate important truths, but stories capture people's hearts. That's why we love novels, biographies, and movies. When I'm in a meeting and someone tells a gripping story about a danger someone courageously faced or a life God changed, people put down their PDAs, stop texting, and sit on the edge of their chairs. It takes time to find and organize a story, but it's preparation time well spent. The leader, though, doesn't have to be the only person to tell stories. In fact, it's often more powerful when team members share stories of God at work to transform individuals and families.

One of Kotter's chief concerns about leaders who want to create a sense of urgency is that they often fail to model it in their own lives. They talk a good game, but there's no fire in their eyes or spring in their steps. Kotter reports, "It is astonishing how many leaders I have seen who say they now 'get it' about urgency, say they understand they must move the troops out of their complacency, and can talk about it correctly, but when you watch them go into their next meeting, their own behavior screams 'everything's fine, no need to worry.' I am amazed at how rare it is for leaders to act with urgency in their own conduct throughout the day. It's as if urgency is just for other people."[4]

Strategy and a commitment to excellence are important, but they can't overcome the daunting obstacle of complacency in a leader's life. Leaders may be able to fake urgency for a while, but not for long. For it to be real and for it to last, urgency has to come from a heart gripped by people's needs and God's grace to meet those needs. Bill Hybels of Willow Creek Community Church talks about the need for God to give leaders a strong sense of "holy discontent" that causes them to be dissatisfied with the status quo and drives them to attempt great things for God. Bob Pierce, the founder of World Vision and Samaritan's Purse, lived with a compelling sense of urgency that came from the heart of

God. He famously pleaded, "Let my heart be broken by the things that break the heart of God." Urgency can be modeled only by leaders who are in touch with God's heart.

Managing Conflict

In my conversations with leaders over the decades, perhaps nothing has robbed them of joy, urgency, and vision as much or as often as enduring conflicts on their staff teams. These challenges threaten to rip the heart out of compassionate leaders, and they create an inordinate share of chaos for a leadership team.

I'm convinced that many church leaders put up with far too much mediocrity and resistance among their staff members. Most of these leaders are compassionate and don't want to upset people by correcting them or demanding compliance with spoken and unspoken norms on the team, but failure to address nagging staff problems creates a stagnant culture at best, and at worst, a toxic one. Actually, I've never consulted with a pastor who didn't need to fire at least one of his staff members. I've heard all the reasons and excuses for keeping resistant, negative people on a team, but I don't buy them. When I hear leaders protest my advice to fire someone, I tell them, "You'll pay a price either way; either a brief and relatively small price by replacing the person, or a much bigger and long-term price if you let the person continue to sour the team and do a poor job in an important ministry area at the church. It's your choice which price you'll pay."

> Living with mediocrity (or worse) on a staff team normalizes ineffectiveness and runs off the best people who want to serve on a team committed to excellence.

When chaos occurs on a staff team, the first thing the leader should do is look at herself and ask some questions: "What am I doing that might be causing this difficulty?" and "What is the pattern here? Is it a long-term, pervasive issue, or an isolated event with a single individual on the team?" The leader may not have given clear directions, defined roles, or facilitated communication among team members. If the conflict or resistance is a single flare-up, the issue is usually resolved fairly easily with good listening, soothed feelings, and clear directions. But too often, conflict on a team is systemic and needs a firm hand. When leaders avoid the hard work of correction, an individual with a negative attitude can cloud the team's ability to communicate effectively and hinder creative ways to touch more people's lives. Living with mediocrity (or worse) on a staff team normalizes ineffectiveness and runs off the best people who want to serve on a team committed to excellence.

To identify mediocre staff members, Paul Idzik, COO of Barclay's Bank, suggests that leaders look for signs of someone who:

Is stubborn and resistant to change Is reactive rather than proactive

Is lazy and unprepared

Makes promises but seldom delivers Shirks responsibility and blames others

Identifies problems without offering solutions[5]

By all means, do everything you can to help struggling staff members find success and fulfillment. Conduct a performance review, be honest about the person's work and attitude, and do everything possible to create a workable, productive situation. There is a wealth of information available on managing staff, so I won't take time to articulate those principles here. There comes a point, however, when we've done all we can do to redeem a staff member, and it hasn't worked. Now it's time to help that person transition as graciously as possible. Provide assistance in helping him find a suitable placement, but don't let your team suffer and God's vision languish any longer.

Having the right staff members and top volunteers is crucial to fulfill a church's vision. Eric O. Long, general manager of the Waldorf Astoria in New York, observes that finding, recruiting, selecting, and placing outstanding staff is becoming more difficult in our society, but good selection yields amazing results. In an interview for *Leaders* magazine, Long observed, "Our organizational development team recently made a presentation to our executive staff, sharing the results of several well-documented studies. It revealed that one great team member has the impact of multiple [mediocre] team members, and in some cases, the ratio was as high as 8:1."[6]

In selecting outstanding staff members, look for more than positive references and experience in certain skills. Dig deeper to uncover the person's passions and commitments. Linda Hudson, president of BAE Systems, offers some pointed suggestions in hiring: "I approach interviews a little differently. The first thing I always ask someone is: 'O.K., I've got your resume. I've been over all the details. Just tell me about your life. Start wherever you want to, from the beginning or the end, but talk to me about you, what you've done, and then walk me through what you've done with your career.' And I found that the way people talk about what matters to them tells me an awful lot about how engaging they are, their energy level, their passion." Hudson is looking for passion, a commitment to excellence, and a good fit. She notes, "I'm looking for the chemistry that would fit well in our environment and how articulate they are. Can they communicate effectively? Do they have that extra something and the passion and people connection that sets them apart from others? What gets you excited? What do you look forward to? Those are the kinds of questions I ask."[7]

When I consult with church leaders about hiring or promoting staff, I suggest they ask four questions:

1. Competence: Can you do the job?

2. Character: Can I trust you?

3. Chemistry: Can you fit in our culture?

4.   Capacity: Can you grow with us?

Two crucial mistakes I've seen in the composition of church leadership teams are keeping mediocre people too long and hiring people too quickly without doing all the homework needed to make a good decision. A good rule to follow is, *make people decisions slowly.* If you rush to hire someone to fill a slot, you may spend countless hours trying to make the person fit, or working through the pain (for everyone) of replacing the person who didn't fit.

Embracing the Chaos of Change

Every team leader knows that some people on the team are more eager to jump on the train of a new idea than others, and there's always someone who drags his feet yelling, "No, it won't work!" up to the day the team celebrates the success of the venture. Leaders need to recognize that people have different degrees of capability to embrace the chaos of change. Perceptive leaders develop the ability to anticipate the response of each person to a challenge or a new opportunity.

To understand people and their responses to change, we need to remember that all of us instinctively ask, "What's in it for me?" Perceptive leaders also learn to ask themselves and their team members two other questions:

1.   What about me embraces or resists this particular change?

2.   What about the culture of our team embraces or resists this change?

An individual may embrace or resist change for any number of reasons: a simple preference, a core value, peer pressure, groupthink, or the need to defend staked-out turf. As I've observed people in times of change, I've noticed that the change itself is often a minor issue in a person's response. The more important factors that shape team members' responses are the way the change is presented, the level of respect for the person who presents it, the rate of change, and the clarity of the team member's role in the process of change. For instance, one team member will gladly embrace any new idea if Susan suggests it because she trusts Susan. If Bill had suggested exactly the same concept, she would have shot it down with a vengeance! Those factors give confidence (or erode it) in the crucial time when people are internalizing the new reality of a changing world.

The Diffusion of Innovations model (popularized by Everett Rogers) helps us understand the terrain of our teams and our churches as we propose change. According to this theory, people adopt one of five roles in their response to change. In my book *What's Shakin' Your Ladder?* I identify these as excited embracers, early embracers, middlers, late embracers, and never embracers. The distribution of these roles in a group forms a bell curve.

- *Excited embracers* make up 2 percent of a population. They are the dreamers and visionaries who are usually recognized as leaders or policymakers.

- *Early embracers* are 18 percent of a group. They are respected and influential, and they eagerly get on board when the concept is explained. Leaders treasure these people on their teams.

- *Middlers* are the largest part of the population, about

- 60 percent of people in the group. They feel more comfortable with the status quo, and they listen very carefully to anyone who resists change. They are willing to get on board only when they are convinced that everybody else will, too.

- *Late embracers* make up 18 percent of the people in a large group. They resist change as long as possible, offering objections all along the way. Eventually, they will go along with the majority, but with a large measure of skepticism and without any enthusiasm at all.

- *Never embracers* are 2 percent of the group. They are steadfastly committed to the past, and they continue to resist change long after the rest of the team is working hard to achieve success.

In most cases, the battle is to win the middlers. You won't need to work hard to convince excited embracers and early embracers of the

> If you can convince the majority of middlers to support the initiative, you are on your way.

value of your new idea. Late embracers won't be convinced until the idea becomes reality, and the never embracers are a lost cause. But if you can convince the majority of middlers to support the initiative, you are on your way.

Most middlers prefer the known to the unknown, the present's certainty to the future's uncertainty. This doesn't mean that middlers are closed to reason or can't catch the excitement of a new vision, but they tend to support the status quo unless they are given a good reason to change. They need to be assured that change won't result in loss of quality and won't cause them to lose their important role on the team.

Make early embracers your allies. Usually they are respected members of the team and the church, so their opinions are given serious consideration, and their leadership is usually followed. Make a list of the early embracers and solicit their active support. Ask them to endorse the new proposal in formal meetings and informal discussions, and enlist their help with the middlers. Explain that hallway and parking lot conversations often influence middlers more than anything else, and let them know that in every meeting, they will make the difference between failure and success. Church leaders don't have any choice about the range of people who attend the church and show up at business meetings. Invariably, late embracers drag their feet and never embracers object to anything and everything. But leaders certainly have the authority and responsibility to select staff members and top volunteers. Careful selection is not an option but a necessity—it makes all the difference in how the team functions, as well as in how (or even if) God's purposes are fulfilled. Look for patterns in people's responses to the chaos of failure or the chaos created by a fresh vision. Some are resistant to only one or two items on the agenda, but others display a pervasive pattern of negativity.

Let me be clear: *know your people.* Give chronically resistant people every opportunity to change, but if they don't change their attitudes in a reasonable amount of time (you'll know), you can't afford to have an anchor on the team holding you back. I don't subscribe to the "convoy theory" that a team moves only as fast as the slowest person. Good leaders have the ability to pull people along more quickly than they would normally move. But leaders shouldn't have anyone on a team who is slower and more resistant than a middler. Of course, we

> Good leaders have the ability to pull people along more quickly than they would normally move.

certainly respect people who ask penetrating questions. That's incredibly valuable to a team! But we need people who ask those questions with an eye toward solutions and a commitment to take bold action when the team has charted a course. Don't settle for anything less.

In times of chaos, leaders need to be observant about the types of responses they can expect from team members, and they need to marshal their primary resources in the organization—the early embracers—to help get others on board with the new plan. Change may be thrust upon the team or the church by outside forces, such as a downturn in the economy or demographic shifts in the community, or high-impact leaders may infuse change into the system by anticipating an opportunity for growth at point A. The leader's response to the chaos of change reflects the current culture, but more important, the experience of chaos offers a perfect classroom to impart a new culture to the team and the body of believers. No matter how well a leader anticipates change and communicates with others, resistance is inevitable. Author and humorist Robert Orben quipped, "Sometimes I get the feeling that the whole world is against me, but deep down I know that's not true. Some of the smaller countries are neutral."

The Value of Honest Feedback

In an open culture that values experimentation and learning, we treasure people who help us reflect more deeply. That's the role Benson

Karanja played in my life when I was president of Beulah Heights University. Benson trusted me enough to challenge my thinking, disagree with me, and help me think more clearly than ever before. He was always willing to ask hard questions, often questions no one else

> Good leaders are observant. They notice what makes people tick, the resources they bring to each issue, and their level of integrity.

was willing to ask out loud, but he didn't ask difficult questions because he wanted to throw up roadblocks. He asked so we could find the very best solutions to the challenges we faced. In our relationship, disagreement wasn't a threat. It only created a context for us to explore and experiment together. All leaders need someone like Benson who is ruthlessly honest, thoroughly good-hearted, willing to patiently probe the depths of an issue, eager to pursue workable solutions, and supportive of the team at every point in the process. I wouldn't be doing what I'm doing today if it weren't for Benson. He is a great gift to me.

People don't bring the same level of insight, skill, and passion to every subject. Some may be passionate about children's ministry, but they couldn't care less about music. In meetings, I've learned to discover what each person brings to the table so that I can appropriately value her for her area of expertise and enthusiasm. In a similar way, some people on the team have more relational and emotional authenticity than others. When perceptive, caring people speak about others' emotional responses to a service or a program, I listen intently to what they have to say. But if the topic of conversation is the budget, I pay close attention to the accountant who has a clear grasp of the numbers, even if he's not relationally perceptive. Good leaders are observant. They notice what makes people tick, the resources they bring to each issue, and their level of integrity.

Chaos—no matter what the cause might be—is a test that shows what people and organizations are really made of. Experiencing times of chaos is like squeezing a sponge: whatever was lurking there before comes out. But seasons of chaos are only tragic if leaders fail to take advantage of them. If we respond with insight, courage, and hope, they become catalysts for incredible growth—for the church and for each person on the team.

Think About It . . .

1. How do you typically respond to failure? How can you help people on your team redefine failure so that it becomes a stepping-stone for growth?

2. Describe the importance of crafting a new vision at point A on the curve instead of waiting until point B. Where are you now in your church or team's life? Do you need to infuse new vision and strategies into your church now? Explain your answer.

3. Who are the early embracers on your team you count on? How can you enlist them more fully to influence the middlers?

7

CHANGING VEHICLES

Reinvent yourself every three years…so that you can remain relevant and able to make new contributions in a world of constant change.…Reinvention is the key to longevity.
—*Stephen R. Covey*

We've seen that changing the culture of a team or a church doesn't happen by magic, and it doesn't happen quickly. It's relatively easy to change a program, but it's more difficult to change the ministry philosophy and strategy that shapes the implementation of a program. But these are relatively easy compared to changing the culture, because culture reflects our most sacred values of integrity, trust, and heart, as well as how we implement our values in every relationship and program. Changing a culture requires clear thinking, concerted effort, enormous courage, and tenacious consistency. But first, we need to recognize what needs to change.

Vision and Vehicle

If I wanted to travel to London from my home in Atlanta, it wouldn't matter if I had a Lamborghini or a Rolls Royce—a car wouldn't get me to Piccadilly. A car could get me to the airport or to a port where I could get on a ship, but a car simply isn't designed to travel across the ocean. No amount of wishing or claiming promises will make the car a suitable vehicle to reach the destination I desire. Now there's absolutely nothing wrong with a car to get me to anywhere on the contiguous land mass. It's perfect for that purpose, but not for ocean travel. If London is my vision, I have to abandon the vehicle I'm using and find another to get me there.

This analogy fits the situation for many church leaders. We may have a very good vehicle (our organizational structure and personnel) to achieve a limited vision, but the one we are currently using may not be able to take us to the place God wants us to go. Like the traveler, no amount of wishing or tinkering with the engine will solve the problem. We can try to put wings on a car, but it still won't fly. We can attach a sail or a rudder to the car, but it won't make the ocean voyage. We need a new vehicle, often a radically new one, if we're going to achieve all that God has for our team and our church. This doesn't make the current vehicle "bad." There's a difference between *bad* and *wrong*. The vehicle we've been using isn't morally deficient or evil in any way. It simply can't produce the results we need. It's the wrong vehicle to take us where we want to go.

When I talk to pastors and explain this principle, they almost always instantly get it. The lights come on in their eyes, and they suddenly realize that they've been trying to drive a car to London! No wonder they've experienced so much frustration. After a few minutes, I often ask, "Now that you see that the vehicle of your organization can't get you to the destination of your vision, which one needs

"Now that you see that the vehicle of your organization can't get you to the destination of your vision, which one needs to change—the vehicle or the destination?"

to change—the vehicle or the destination?" This may seem like a simplistic, rhetorical question, but actually, it's crucial. When leaders keep butting their heads against a wall day after day—or, using our metaphor, they keep driving up to the beach on the East Coast and realizing they can't go any farther toward London—many of them scale back their vision to match the capabilities of their organizational vehicle. That's precisely the wrong solution! When they finally realize how their existing structure and personnel aren't capable of achieving their vision, their frustration melts into a firm conviction to do the only reasonable thing: change the vehicle.

When I meet with pastors and discuss the principle of creating an organizational vehicle to fulfill their vision, I want to find out if their vision is clear and strong, and I want to help them see if their organizational structure and people can take them to reach that vision. Dr. Gerald Brooks (www.growingothers.com) has helped me think through this issue by using a series of test questions.

1. The heart test: Is the vision burning brightly in the heart of the leader, both in public descriptions of where God is leading him and passionately in his heart?

2. The leadership test: Do the top leaders in the church share this vision, or are they apathetic or resistant? Are these the people who can take the church to the vision's destination?

3. The organization test: How well does the current organizational structure work to achieve the vision? What are the bottlenecks? Which aspects are cars that can't take you there? Which ones are planes or ships?

4. The recruiting test: Are new hires and volunteers on board with the vision, or are they still a work in progress?

5. The message test: Is the vocabulary of the vision consistent and strong in every part of the church? Is the message of the vision reflected in sermons, written materials, the budget, signs, and conversations about the priorities of the church?

6. The planning test: Is the church's vision your staff's benchmark for strategic planning in every area?

7. The facility test: Do facilities, including their layout, design, and decor, reflect the vision?

8. The money test: Does the budget demonstrate the vision's priorities?

9. The pragmatism test: Does the vision make sense? Is it both God-sized and workable? Can you see it happening? Is it so global that it doesn't capture anyone's heart, or is it appropriately targeted?

10. The capacity test: How well does the capacity of the current organizational structure and personnel match the vision?

11. The clarity test: Can people throughout the organization articulate the vision clearly and with passion? If you ask people who come out the door after the service on Sunday morning to articulate the vision of the church, could they share it clearly and with enthusiasm?

12. The counsel test: Who are the outside voices that are helping to shape the vision and the vehicle to fulfill it?

13. The growth test: How do the ministries of the church need to be organized to capitalize on the next two stages of growth?

How do we know if a vision is from God? One of the measures is that it has to be something so big that it requires God's wisdom and power to pull it off. Anything less is just a good idea. God's vision is to redeem not only individuals but the entire creation. He's not just making new men and women; He's going to re-create the entire universe in the New Heaven and New Earth. That's a big vision! Small visions don't enflame people's hearts—yours or those who follow you.

> If your vision is from God, it will blow your socks off and keep you awake at night!

Don't dumb down your vision to be something that isn't threatening. If your vision is from God, it will blow your socks off and keep you awake at night! People instinctively understand the power of a big, compelling vision. When he was an old man, English sculptor Henry Moore was asked, "Now that you are 80, you must know the secret of life. What is it?"

Moore smiled and answered, "The secret of life is to have a task, something you do your entire life, something you bring everything to, every minute of the day for your whole life. And the most important thing is: It must be something you cannot possibly do."[1] That's a good benchmark for our visions, too.

Some churches are rocking along pretty well. They have a bold, clear vision, and they enjoy a culture of creativity and experimentation, so their people are conditioned to embrace new ideas. Many churches, though, have been doing the same things so long that they don't even know other vehicles exist. To change the metaphor, these leaders need to heal the infection before they can perform a heart transplant. If they attempt surgery before they've dealt with the infection, the patient— their team and their church—will suffer and die. The first step for them is to get the body as healthy as possible, and then take bold steps to change the culture.

Clarity, Congruence, and Courage

When Raymond heard me speak at a conference, he asked to meet with me for breakfast the next morning. After we got to know each other for a few minutes, he began to pour out his frustrations. "Dr. Chand, I have no idea how our church got to this point, but I feel like I'm spending most of my time on things that weren't the reason we began the church eight years ago. Can you help me sort this out?"

"I'll certainly try," I assured him.

Raymond's eyes lit up as he described how the church began. He and his team believed that God called them to reach unchurched people in the suburbs of New York. "We didn't have to look very far to find unbelievers," he said with a smile.

I asked, "How did things go the first few years?"

He sat back in his chair and shook his head with a big grin. "It was incredible. We saw so many people saved, so many families reunited. I loved every minute of it."

"What happened?" I asked him. "What has caused your disappointment since then?"

"Somewhere along the way, we started doing good things instead of the best things." I knew exactly what he meant, but I asked him to continue. "As more people came to Christ, we began discipling them. Soon, people wanted us to have a family life center, and before long, we had a bowling alley and a coffee shop."

"These weren't part of the vision God gave you?" I probed.

Raymond shook his head again, but this time without a smile. "I thought they were, and people assured me they were, but in the past few years, we've invested far more time, money, and people into things like the bowling alley than reaching people for Christ." He paused, then told me, "I'm not sure what to do now. I feel like we've missed what God called us to do, but there seems to be no turning back."

"You can always do what God called you to do, Raymond. But you're right. You're going to have to unravel some good things so you can devote yourself to the best. It'll be hard, but God will give you the wisdom to do it."

> You're going to have to unravel some good things so you can devote yourself to the best.

Many leaders have faced similar circumstances. They joined a church with a passionate vision, but over time, the vision atrophied or shifted to something else. Let me explain the difference between the dining area of a fine restaurant and the restaurant's kitchen. When I take my wife to a lovely restaurant, we enjoy the nice tablecloth, flowers, soft music, gentle lighting, courteous service, and wonderful meal. But a few inches beyond that idyllic setting is a very different environment: the kitchen. That's where people are running around cooking, preparing plates, and fussing with each other so that they can provide the perfect dinner for my wife and me. In the same way, when people come to a church's worship service, they enjoy the best and the most beautiful setting we can provide. Sometimes they say to each other, "Wow, I'd love to work in a place like this. It's wonderful!" But they have no idea that the real work of the church is much more like the kitchen, and they are shocked to find that making a delicious entree is a messy process. Leading a church isn't much different from being a chef in a busy, chaotic kitchen.

Quite often, ministry leaders and board members have offered ideas, suggestions, and plans that sounded great, but may not have been in alignment with the original vision. The leader didn't want to discourage the creativity of those people, so he smiled and went along. "It can't hurt anything, can it?" he wondered. But eventually the leader wakes up and realizes that too many compromises have been made and that the organization's vision is significantly different from his own. To remedy the conflict, too many leaders conclude that it's easier to adjust their own sense of God's calling and vision than to expend all the energy it would require to bring the entire leadership team, plans, and programs back into alignment with the original vision.

Maybe he's tired. Maybe he's discouraged. Maybe he's tired of fighting and feeling alone, and maybe he realizes all too well that it will be a colossal struggle to turn the team around. But if he continues to give in and support a vision he doesn't really believe in, he's not being true to himself, to God, or to his people. The leader has subordinated his God-given vision to a group of people who are taking the church to a different place. The conflict probably isn't between good and evil. Their vision and their destination are probably noble and worthy, too, but the pastor has to own a vision, not acquiesce to someone else's. We're not talking about a dictatorship or a heavy-handed style. We're talking about the importance—the necessity—of visionary leadership. The members of the team must be in line with the leader's vision and core values. If they aren't, he can't lead them. A pastor can't chart a course, plan effectively, and motivate his troops if his people aren't on board with his vision and core values. Organizational congruence is necessary if staff members are going to achieve God's vision and work effectively as a team. Without it, there's only confusion and conflict.

> A pastor can't chart a course, plan effectively, and motivate his troops if his people aren't on board with his vision and core values.

When a leader's vision and values are aligned with the organization's goals and the hearts of the team members, the congruence will be reflected in everything they do. For example, a local Atlanta church states that one of its core values is missions. This value is demonstrated in planning, budgeting, personnel, and even in prayer. The budget shows a large percentage of the church's income going to mission projects, and the missions department has more staff members and volunteers than any other department in the church. A glance at the church calendar shows that it's peppered with missions-related activities. Missionaries, mission trips, and mission funding and prayer are high priorities on the pastor's schedule, too. This focus demonstrates organizational congruence at the church around a compelling vision.

As I've worked with church leaders, I've observed them moving through the following phases as they've implemented new strategies, especially in changing their cultures:

1. Entrepreneurial, or the *discovery* phase, when the strategy is seen as viable: it can be done!

2. Emerging, or the *growth* phase, when credibility is crucial: the leader can be trusted.

3. Established, or the *maintenance* phase, when stability is achieved: the systems are in place and functioning well.

4. Eroding, or the *survival* phase, when the church is vulnerable: signs of decline are obvious.

5. Enterprising, or the *reinvention* phase, when leaders adapt to a fresh vision and new strategies: they adjust so they can grow again.

The only way to avoid eroding is to keep going back to being entrepreneurial. When leaders rest on their past successes, they become organizationally flabby—soft and passive. In fact, the more successful an organization has been in the past, the more likely it is to fail in the future. Without the constant infusion of entrepreneurial spirit, flourishing can lead to floundering!

Churches must "re-dream" the dream or discover a new compelling vision for their existence. For a leadership team and those they lead to continue developing and growing, they must focus on the organizing principles of the stages ahead. Leadership styles and the key issues to be addressed are different for each stage of the cycle. Effective leaders understand the cycle and are able to adapt their leadership to the corresponding needs of each stage.

> Churches must "re-dream" the dream or discover a new compelling vision for their existence.

The danger is that the old mental models will remain in place and that the desire for the security and familiarity of the past will win out over the opportunity of the moment to embrace and live out a new dream. Your thoughts will create your attitude, which leads to action. The Chinese characters that form the word *crisis* are a combination of *danger* and *opportunity*. Every crisis calls us to face danger, but we need to redefine it as opportunity. Olan Hendrix, author of *Three Dimensions of Leadership*, observed, "Generally, religious organizations start out with a goal orientation...deteriorate to a task orientation...and finally degenerate to a bottom-line control organization." Don't let that happen to you!

Your effectiveness will always depend on your ability to see the future. To be an effective leader, you must understand the difference between *change* and *transition*. *Change* is the event (for example, the first vision is realized, the founding pastor is gone, the community demographics have changed), and *transition* is the emotional, psychological, and social response to that change. In most situations, not enough attention is paid to the transition side, and leaders often move forward without realizing that the congregation, staff, or both are not processing the change at the same level they are.

Your future can be bright if:

+ You have a compelling vision.

+ You have aligned the resources and ministries of the church to the vision.

+ You understand the process of change and transition.

+ You have the blessing of the Lord.

Strategic planning needs to be written in pencil because in a dynamic, changing environment, strategic planning needs constant evaluation and adjustment.

Congruence is a key component of an effective organizational vehicle. It is clear focus that organizes people, plans, and funding, and it flows from the church's vision, mission, and core values, permeating every department of the church. Of course, some churches do a better job than others, but the fact is, most leadership teams never even consider the importance of congruence. They just think, talk, and plan the way they've always done. The results are pockets of wonderful success, with some department leaders competing with others for resources, and some apathetic about

> The organization can't fulfill a God-sized vision, even in its local market, without the alignment of people, plans, and funding around a common purpose.

what happens in other parts of the church. The absence of congruence is like a plane with one wing missing, a ship without a rudder, or a car with a flat tire. The organization can't fulfill a God-sized vision, even in its local market, without the alignment of people, plans, and funding around a common purpose.

Congruence and Strategic Planning

An old adage says that the devil is in the details, but actually, I believe that the fulfillment of a vision is in the details. Global statements have a place, but they need to be backed up with specific, strategic plans to fulfill the vision. Developing a healthy culture is the "soft side" of leadership, but strategic planning, the "hard side" of leadership, is also essential. The two complement each other. When staff members and church attendees hear concrete plans designed to accomplish the church's purpose, they trust their leaders, and the culture takes a step forward. If, however, they always hear glowing vision statements without seeing how the vision is going to be realized, they become skeptical of their leaders. Stagnant, discouraging, and toxic cultures usually aren't short on vision. In fact, their leaders often communicate grand and glorious pictures of the future. Many of these cultures are unhealthy because their leaders don't back up their lofty words with specific plans. Their people soon learn that they are full of hot air.

Strategic planning enables a team and every department in the church to work together for a common goal. It's the hallmark of congruence, and it's essential to healthy church cultures. For example, a pastor explained to me that he wanted to grow the children's ministry at his church. The church's vision statement is "Bringing families to the church." The pastor and his staff didn't just hope people would come to their church so that their families could experience God's grace. They did their homework to study the specific demographics of their community, and they began formulating their plans around the opportunities they found. They learned that a lot of children lived in apartments near the church. Many of these children lived in single-parent homes. The pastor and his staff talked about the emotional, relational, financial, and spiritual needs of these parents and their kids. One of the staff members in the children's ministry had coordinated a program for this demographic group at a church a few years before. Another person called a friend who served at a church across the country, a church that had a large and successful ministry to single parents and their kids.

The pastor and his team didn't rush to create a program. They carefully studied the demographics, talked to people with successful ministries, and read books and articles on the subject. After several weeks of study, reflection, and conversation, they were ready to dive into the planning process. They began with the existing vision and discussed how this idea of reaching families was congruent with this vision. As they dug down deeper, their questions became increasingly specific. The process they used included these elements:

Crucial Questions

+ What is our church's vision?

+ What is the need we see in people's lives? How does meeting this need relate to our vision and core values? (Is there congruence with the vision?)

+ Who will be responsible for this plan and this ministry? How will the implementation of the plans enhance or detract from existing activities and priorities? Is this price worth paying? Why or why not? Do the responsible people have a passion to meet these needs?

+ What are the specific elements of the plan to accomplish this goal?

+ What are the due dates for specific tasks, and who will accomplish them? What are the benchmarks of progress in the next month, six months, year, and two years?

+ How much will the plan cost, including people, materials, facilities, funding, and other resources?

+ Do we have the capacity to undertake this right now? If not, what needs to happen to increase capacity? What is the threshold for taking the plan from the conceptual stage to implementation?

+ How will we measure success?

After the team walked through the planning process (which took three weeks to complete), they reviewed their plans to be sure that all team members were on the same page. The pastor reiterated the church's vision statement, shared the results of the team's research, and stated the overall plan to reach families in the community with a new strategy. Then he asked the group, "Just to be crystal clear about our plans, why are we doing this?"

The children's ministry coordinator responded, "Because over 70 percent of the local families have children, and if we can reach the children, we can reach the rest of their families."

"Who is going to do it?"

An associate pastor looked across the table and nodded, "Annette is our children's coordinator, and she'll be responsible for it."

"How will she do it?"

Annette replied, "After looking at all the options, our team is going to use a programming plan that worked at a church in Oregon."

"How much will it cost?" the pastor asked.

Annette answered, "Each program will have a deadline and a budget associated with it."

"Annette, who will you be accountable to?"

Everyone laughed and pointed back at the pastor. He smiled and responded, "You're right. She'll report directly to me. We will evaluate her progress monthly and base it on the growth in the number of children enrolled in church school, children's church, and special activities, and we'll track to see if the new people who attend are from our target area. We also plan to have an annual review, and we will attach separate goals for that review."

When a team learns the principles of strategic planning and gains some experience, it becomes second nature for them to value the congruence of vision, people, and resources.

Strategic planning is an acquired skill. When a team learns the principles of strategic planning and gains some experience, it becomes second nature for them to value the congruence of vision, people, and resources. A healthy, powerful culture moves a team and a church body toward the ultimate objectives God has given them.

I've noticed that many leaders don't have a framework for decision making. They just do whatever looks best at the moment. Perhaps the simplest and clearest template for planning is to follow the acronym SMART. Plans need to be *s*pecific, *m*easurable, *a*ccountable, *r*easonable, and *t*imely.

When presented with a complicated decision that could change the direction of the organization and shape the culture, we need to ask four questions; and it is important that we ask them in this order.

1. *Is the program in line with our vision, mission, and core values?* No matter how great an idea or opportunity, if the program isn't in line with the vision, we must say no to it. Most church leaders use their vision statements to say yes, but they rarely use it to say no and eliminate options. If everything imaginable fits under the umbrella of the vision, perhaps the vision statement is too broad and needs to be refined and clarified.

2. *Do we have the organizational and human capacity—and the heart—to do this?* The program may be so large that it creates enormous stress for the entire team, or perhaps we don't have the right people on the team to accomplish the objective, our

facilities and volunteer manpower are not be adequate to achieve the goals, or it's just not the right time.

3. *How will God be glorified?* Most leaders will ask, "Will God be glorified?" and the answer is almost always yes. When the answer is always yes, we are probably asking the wrong question. Instead, ask, "How?" This question will help us understand the true impact the decision will have on God's kingdom.

4. *How much will it cost?* This must be the last question asked. Understand the true nature of this question, and then consider it carefully. It's not "Can we afford it?" Most churches and nonprofit organizations don't have piles of money sitting around waiting to be used. The initial answer to the question of affordability is usually no. But the answer to "How much will it cost?" is different. The cost includes not only dollars but also people, resources, time, and energy pulled from other projects and programs. Most churches didn't come this far in their history because they had plenty of resources, but because their leaders were resourceful. It's not about resources; it's about being resourceful. A program that is immediately blocked by the question "Can we afford it?" might get a different response after asking all four questions. If the vision is big enough, if the people have a heart for doing it, if God will be glorified in a specific way, then the money will come.

Answering these specific questions *in this order* helps us grasp the nature of the opportunity in front of us. Then we can make principled decisions based on a larger organizational context, not on a situation, such as the amount of cash in the bank account. Using these four questions to train leaders and teams in decision making has proven to be tremendously helpful. The discussion enabled them to know why they made a particular decision, why they rejected a course of action, and why they deferred a choice until later. The four-question grid gives teams direction and confidence as they consider any decision, from the largest to the smallest issues they face.

Passengers in the Vehicle

When things aren't working, leaders often prefer to change the structure of an organization because it is the easiest area to tackle. Moving boxes around on an organizational chart, reassigning who reports to whom, and handing out new titles don't rock many boats. Restructuring is a clean process, and it seems to offer the biggest gain at the least cost. In most organizations, however, reorganizing the structure doesn't make people work better or harder. This reminds me of the man who needs to clean out his garage but decides to organize his bedroom closet because it's easier. He may get finished more quickly and he may not get as dirty, but he won't have a clean garage.

Changing the organizational structure doesn't change an individual's motivation, behavior, values, or way of relating to others. Changing the culture—the way people relate to each other and their commitments—or changing the people are the only ways to see real progress. To change things in an organization, it's far more important to make adjustments to the informal connections, not the formal structure. These informal processes are the ways people communicate, make decisions, and support or hinder each other. These are far harder to identify and address than moving a box on an organizational chart, but they promise far greater rewards. We need to set the standard very high for our staff members. The stakes are far too high for us to settle for less. God has called us to partner with Him to redeem the world, and like Jesus, we are willing to work with anyone who responds. As we consider our leadership teams, however, we need to continually raise the bar. Staff members who can't or won't become part of a supportive, reflective, visionary culture shouldn't be allowed to poison it. Larry Bossidy, chairman and CEO of Honeywell, remarked, "People have told me I spend too much time on people, but I know that if I get the best people, I am

> Changing the organizational structure doesn't change an individual's motivation, behavior, values, or way of relating to others.

going to walk away with the prize. In this day and age, organizations that don't have the best people don't win." People must take priority over structure.

Jim Baker is executive pastor of Brentwood Baptist Church in Brentwood, Tennessee. He notes, "In the midst of rapid growth, we have learned that organizational clarity, alignment, and collaboration are everything. In fact, we have learned that our effectiveness is ultimately the result of how well we execute these three critical processes. [These have] helped create a culture of shared purpose and achieve consistent levels of peak performance." Baker and his team have worked hard to make sure they have congruence among the staff's roles, the church's vision, and their strategic plans. "Establishing this culture is not easy," he relates, "and every church and organization must find its own way. But the outcome is worth the effort. Supervisors will spend less time fretting over what their [staff members] are doing and more time focusing on the future of the ministry. Employees and volunteers will know what to do and feel empowered to do it. And everyone will be excited, surprised and delighted with extraordinary results."[2]

Changing from one vehicle to another always creates chaos for a team. It's inevitable. The patterns of roles, expectations, reporting, and lines of communication that have been so familiar are now analyzed, and many are changed. Sometimes pastors realize they need to change vehicles at the moment when their church experiences a huge growth spurt. I consulted with a pastor who moved his church from a three-thousand-seat auditorium to one that holds over seven thousand. In the months leading up to the move, he assured me that he had prepared his staff and everything was under control. A month after the move, he told me, "The moment we moved into the new building, 80 percent of my staff proved to be inadequate for their new roles. We simply hadn't prepared them. We've had to scramble to equip them for the new expectations. Some are going to do fine, but a few aren't going to make the change. I thought I could just put new tires on the old vehicle and we'd reach our vision's destination that way, but now I realize that I was thinking way too small." Over the next few months, this pastor led his team in demolishing the old vehicle and creating one that promised to take them where God was leading them.

Steps of Transition

People often say they "are afraid of" change or they "don't like" change, but in my observation, most people are far more afraid of the process of the transition from one team to another, one plan to another, or one leader to another than they are afraid of the actual change itself. Many leaders focus on changing the external in their

> Many leaders focus on changing the external in their church world, but changing a culture rivets our attention on the deeper internal issues: relationships, values, and other matters of the heart.

church world, but changing a culture rivets our attention on the deeper internal issues: relationships, values, and other matters of the heart. To be a good pastor or team leader, it isn't enough only to think through what you're going to do. You must also take time to consider all of the contingencies and write a comprehensive transitional plan.

In the previous example of the pastor and his leadership team developing a strategic plan for the children's ministry, the next step in the planning process would be to make a list of all possible challenges and changes. For example, how would Annette's priorities change? Would some of her responsibilities shift to someone else, or would the church suspend those programs?

New plans always have a ripple effect in altering priorities, schedules, budgets, and, perhaps, reporting relationships in several levels of the organization. Even if only the children's ministry is directly affected by major transitions in the new strategy, the people in every other component of the church's life need to understand how the change will affect them. To minimize surprises, the team, and especially the team most involved with the changes, needs to anticipate these ripples and consider possible contingencies. If the new plan isn't carefully thought through, people in the organization may be confused and wonder about the credibility of the decision makers. Credibility is a people problem, but it's not the only relational problem to consider during a transition. The main question is, How does a leader position each team member for success?

After thinking about this question, the leader can create a written plan and then make decisions based on the plan. For example, she can ask herself these questions:

How will I approach each person?

How will I communicate the details of changes in priorities, budget, schedule, and reporting to this individual?

What information will that person need to understand this change?

You can be sure that different people will have very different perceptions of every new direction, and even if you explain things very carefully, some of them will disagree. That's especially true when you need to remove someone from a high-profile position. I talked to a pastor who told me that his worship leader confessed to viewing pornography. He didn't confess, though, until someone saw explicit images on his computer in his church office. The pastor wanted to save this man's reputation and protect his wife's feelings as much as possible, so he let him quietly resign. When staff members found out how the pastor handled the situation, they were polarized: the women were furious because they believed that the pastor should have publicly rebuked the worship leader as an example to the flock, but most of the men felt that the pastor had been too hard on him. It was, after all, the first time he'd been caught viewing porn. When some of the students learned what was going on, they wondered what the big deal was about. Some of the older people in the church wanted to lynch him!

This was a classic transitional challenge. Moving him out of his role as worship leader was a simple, straightforward change, but the transitional issues of communication and community understanding proved to be very difficult. In my experience, transitional difficulties are quite predictable when staff are fired.

In every major transition in a church, leaders need to be alert, and they must anticipate all the contingencies and make plans to deal with each one of them—knowing that some of these plans will be implemented, but most won't be needed.

William Bridges, a noted expert on change and transition, explains in his most recent book, *Managing Transitions: Making the Most of Change*, that the reason change agents fail is that they focus on the solution instead of the problem. This may seem counterintuitive to forward-thinking, visionary leaders, but Bridges teaches that people need to be gripped by the need before they will embrace the solution. In fact, he believes that 90 percent of a leader's efforts should be spent on selling the problem and helping people understand what is *not* working. He rightly claims that people don't perceive the need for a solution if they don't fully grasp the problem.

I've listened to countless pastors explain their vision to me, to a group of pastors, or to their congregations. Most of them focus their attention on the benefits they will enjoy when God fulfills a particular objective in their church and community. Comparatively few of them take time to paint the picture of people's needs so that hearts are stirred. When people are touched by pain, heartache, and lostness in others' lives, they'll

> When people are touched by pain, heartache, and lostness in others' lives, they'll eagerly embrace solutions to meet those needs.

eagerly embrace solutions to meet those needs. That's the power of organizations like World Vision and Compassion International. They don't just ask people for money for kids. Before they mention money, they show the faces of children who live in poverty and ignorance, and only then do they show how a person's contribution can effectively change a child's life. Is this manipulative? Not in the least. It's simply the most effective way to move the hearts of people so that they want to participate in meeting the needs of hurting people.

Good planning is essential in creating a positive culture, and it works at all times with all people. When I resigned from Beulah Heights University, I traveled all over the country to meet with board members and tell them what I was going to do and why. I was recommending Benson Karanja as my successor. In making that change, I had a transition plan. I knew the people I was going to talk to, when I was going to talk to them, and what I was going to say. The time spent thinking and planning for this transition made what could have been a painful time for me and the school into a very positive learning experience for everyone involved.

The responsibility for a successful transition is in the hands of the leader making the change. In one of my seminars, a young woman named Regina said she was moved from a minor role in the children's department to a larger responsibility as minister of Christian education. Regina did everything she could to prepare her people for a change. She found and trained her successor and helped transition her old team to their new leader. But no one helped pave the way for Regina's transition to her new role. The pastor failed to make an announcement to the church that Regina was given this new responsibility. And even worse, the former Christian education minister wasn't informed that he was now out of a job, so he continued in his position as if nothing had changed. This was a change without a transition. Regina had made the change, but without her pastor helping with the transition, she was now impotent in her new responsibility.

Some might wonder why a pastor would be so neglectful. I have a little more information that brings light to the situation. Regina is the pastor's daughter, and he was worried about how people would react to his giving her such an important role. He believed that she was the best person for the job, and she felt that she was ready, but his poor communication of the transition kept the church from having confidence in her. As you can imagine, this pastor created quite a mess. He had to deal with both a personal conflict—after all, she's his daughter—and professional challenges: he needed to resolve conflict on two teams and between two staff members who had been assigned the same role. But the pastor wasn't very quick to resolve these problems. When I first heard about the situation, Regina had been in her job for three months!

My recommendation to the pastor was to make a clear pronouncement to his people: "My daughter, Regina, is going to provide great leadership to the Christian education ministry department at our church. Actually, she should have been functioning in this position for the last three months, but I have been remiss in not making that announcement. I'm correcting that today. Come on up here, Regina, and tell them about your vision. What's God going to do through you and your team?"

> Assimilating people into leadership roles is one of the most difficult challenges we face.

Assimilating people into leadership roles is one of the most difficult challenges we face. However, if we properly prepare and execute a transition plan, and if we take responsibility for the changes we institute, we'll build trust, provide clear direction, and reinforce a positive culture.

Transitions in a Team's Culture

Some of us look at the size of our church and conclude that it's impossible to make any difference in its culture. The vehicle of organizational structure and personnel is, we're convinced, what it is, and it will always be the same. We've been to conferences, prayed, and talked to other leaders until our tongues hang out, but nothing has changed. Before we give up completely and fade into passive resentment of leaders or followers (depending on our position), we need to understand that our role in implementing change should be focused only on those immediately around us. We don't need to fret about everybody, but we can take bold steps to make a difference in the culture of our own teams. In an article in *Leader to Leader*, Dave Logan, John King, and Halee Fisher-Wright identify smaller clusters of people they call "tribes." A small organization may have only one tribe, but large churches and other corporate entities might contain hundreds or even thousands of tribes. The authors observe that changing a tribe's culture from toxic to inspiring follows five distinct stages. Change doesn't happen by trying to jump two or three stages at once, but instead by slowly and carefully building trust and authenticity to move up one stage at a time.[3]

Using the language of our scale of five types of culture, the authors report:

+ About 2 percent of tribes are toxic. They create and perpetuate a poisonous environment like a street gang. Life, they are convinced, is totally unfair, and each person is left to dominate or to defend himself at all costs.

+ Following a bell curve, 25 percent of tribes are discouraging. People perceive themselves as hopeless victims who have no power (and no responsibility) to change the atmosphere.

+ Approximately half of all organizations are composed of stagnant tribes. Here, effort is expended on achieving personal success, personal advancement, and personal gain. In these tribes, people are divided into the "haves" who are beating the system and the "have-nots" who aren't making the progress they desire. The words "I," "me," and "my" dominate conversations.

+ Accepting tribes are found in 22 percent of organizations. In these productive and supportive environments, shared values and teamwork focus attention on the common goals of the group.

+ Only 2 percent of tribal cultures inspire people to devote their shared energies to creative solutions aimed at achieving the seemingly impossible. This kind of culture is rare, and it is also quite vulnerable to slipping back to a state of reduced creativity, confused values, and selfish ambitions.

Senior pastors can work hard to take all the tribes in their churches on a journey from where they are to become inspiring communities, but the first step is to work on their own leadership team. And the rest of the staff members need to realize that they can't change the whole culture of the organization, but can take their own teams on a journey from one stage to the next. There is no magic bullet to transform a team into an inspiring culture overnight. Those who try to make that happen frustrate themselves and disappoint their teams. To see change in a team's culture, the first step is to take a good, hard look at our own perceptions, attitudes, and behaviors. Change begins with us.

Healthy cultures thrive because the right people are in the right roles sharing a common vision and working with congruent plans, priorities, and resources. All these elements are essential. As we've seen, too many leaders put up with less than healthy cultures because they aren't willing to pay the price to destroy the old and create the new. Changing an unhealthy culture to a strong, vibrant one requires both

> Too many leaders put up with less than healthy cultures because they aren't willing to pay the price to destroy the old and create the new.

a sledgehammer and a potter's wheel. We have to be ruthless to attack systems (not people) that block us from achieving our new objectives, but we also need to carefully mold a new culture with gentleness, wisdom, and strength—like a skilled potter making a beautiful vase.

Good leaders ruthlessly wield sledgehammers to destroy inadequate organizational vehicles, but they pull out a wider range of tools to use with people. Team members are closely tied to the old structures, so it's wise to use the right tool to communicate effectively with each staff member. I've known some who needed only a light tap to shatter old thinking and get them into the new vehicle, but I've also had to use a twenty-pound sledgehammer to make a dent with a few people. My goal in all cases isn't to hurt them, but to help them make the transition from the old to the new. And all along, I've painted pictures as clearly as possible to show them what we're missing, capture their hearts by showing them the needs of people, and show how they play a crucial role in the new vehicle. Communicating clearly and powerfully is my responsibility. I explain that each of us "has to give up a little to go up a lot." If I've observed them very well, I can anticipate how each one will respond, and I know how big a tap I need to make to help that individual let go of the old way of doing things and take steps toward a new, stronger, more effective vehicle.

One of the most interesting questions to ask leaders is, Who are the real power brokers in your meetings? At first, most of them will say, "Well, I am." They have the title and the role, but quite often, the informal power is owned by a sour person who fills the room with doubts, or a person who sees every decision through the grid of money instead of God's calling, or someone who demands that everyone agree with him on any subject. When these people (and these are just a few examples) are given informal power in a meeting, moving forward is as hard as pushing a rope uphill. This kind of culture has to be crushed so that a positive one can be created.

In these times of transition, people often become territorial—precisely at the time we want them to be more open to working as a team. In a meeting, for example, if a ministry leader insists on clinging to a room assignment because that's where and when one of her groups has met for years, but I've asked her to make an adjustment, I first go to that person privately and say something like this: "Beth, I know that group is important to you and it's inconvenient to ask them to meet at another time, but I need you to help me think and plan for the whole church, not just for your department. Can you do that for me?" Usually, that's enough, just a light tap, and she gets on board. But if she still resists my direction in the next meeting, I turn to her with a heavier hammer and say, "Beth, I've noticed that every time we have conversations about making the transitions we've been discussing, you want to protect your department from any changes. Your department is very important to all of us, but we are all making some tradeoffs to make this work. I need for you to work with the rest of us. We've talked about this privately.

Resistance to change bogs us down and takes our attention away from where we need to go. Can I count on you from this point forward?" Then I turn to the rest of the group and say, "Now, where were we?" And we continue our meeting.

When leaders face transitions like those described in this chapter, they often instinctively ask, "How much am I going to bleed when I go through this?" But that's the wrong question. A better question is, "I know I'm going to bleed. How can I help my team get healthy as quickly as possible?" When a surgeon has to amputate a man's leg, does the man want her to use a scalpel or a butter knife? If she uses the butter knife, she'll eventually get the leg off, but the process will be very messy. The biggest risk for a patient with a diseased leg is to avoid surgery, and if you wait until you're 100 percent sure that surgery is necessary, it's probably too late and the patient will die. If surgery is needed, the patient will do best if a skilled surgeon uses the sharpest scalpel she can find. That's the way to get the operation over as quickly as possible and protect the health of the patient. If you have to fire three people on your team, you and the rest of your team will bleed far more if you fire them one at a time over several months.

> In healthy cultures where skilled, caring leaders communicate often and well with their teams and value their input, risks are minimized because people feel affirmed, have clear roles and goals, and don't become embroiled in turf wars.

In healthy cultures where skilled, caring leaders communicate often and well with their teams and value their input, risks are minimized because people feel affirmed, have clear roles and goals, and don't become embroiled in turf wars. But in unhealthy cultures, almost every interaction carries the risk of increasing levels of misunderstanding and distrust.

Don't put up with a deficient vehicle any longer. Destroy what you need to destroy, and create something beautiful in its place. The sledgehammer, though, has to be used with precision. Destroy possessive turf wars on your team; take the hammer to decisions that are based solely on money instead of vision; hit the spirit of blaming others and being exclusive; and obliterate the spirit of secret alliances, suspicion, and distrust. The free CULTURE survey (www.samchandculture survey.com) will surface elements that need attention in your environment. When you see them, take a deep breath, think carefully, and pray deeply, then pick up your sledgehammer and begin destroying any unhealthy segments as you create a new culture for your team and your church.

Think About It . . .

1. Will your current vehicle (organizational structure and personnel) take you to the destination of your church's vision? Why or why not?

2. Describe the level of congruence of your church in the areas of a shared vision, a common ministry philosophy and strategy, and the use of resources. In what areas is there conflict or passive acceptance instead of eager support for one another?

3. What's the role of strategic planning in creating a new vehicle that will get you where you believe God wants you to go?

4. How does (or will) the process of thinking through the contingencies help you navigate the transitional issues as you develop a new vehicle?

8

YES, YOU CAN!

I've missed more than 9000 shots in my career. I've lost almost 300 games.
Twenty-six times I've been trusted to take the winning shot and missed.
I've failed over and over again in my life. And that is why I succeed.
—Michael Jordan

Is it possible to transform a culture? Some of us think that it seems almost too good to be true. But yes, it's not only possible but also the most productive work we can do because it has a dramatic, multiplied impact—on the team, in the church, and throughout the community.

If Scott Can . . .

If Scott Wilson can change his culture, anyone can. Scott joined the staff of his father's church in South Dallas as the youth pastor, and God used him in marvelous ways. Before long, the board and his father asked him to be the co-pastor of the church. This arrangement was an honor, but it proved to be quite awkward for everyone involved.

Years before, Scott's father, Tom, had come to the church as the pastor and as the superintendent of the church's private school. The church had been one of the most prestigious in the denomination, but it had declined in recent years, and the school was in financial trouble. It had borrowed $75,000 to pay overdue utility bills to keep the lights on and the doors open, but it ran a $100,000 deficit each year. Tom is a gifted leader, but he had walked into a hornet's nest. The church and school didn't have clear delineation. They shared finances and shared staff, which initially sounded like a good idea, but soon led to enormous headaches. The future looked grim for both the church and the school. Something had to be done, and done quickly. Tom and his board closed the school, but a large number of families were incensed at the decision and left the church. The remnant could barely support the church and the now almost empty worship center. In fact, things got so bad that they considered closing not only the school but the church, too.

Adding Scott as the youth pastor gave the ministry a shot in the arm. South Dallas is a rough area with rampant gang violence and related crimes. Under Scott's leadership, however, gang members came to Christ, attendance grew, and hundreds of lives were changed. But the specter of the past haunted Tom, Scott, and the church. Several board members were still bitterly disappointed that the school had been closed, and they blamed Tom. He spent those first years trying to rebuild the board and the trust with those who stayed.

Heartache, though, wasn't relegated to turf wars on the board. The youth ministry was strong and growing, but tragedy threatened to derail it. Many students in that part of the city were involved in gangs, including some students who were part of Scott's ministry. One night, a young man was killed in a drive-by shooting. Two of his friends were young men who had joined rival gangs, and one of them wanted revenge. He invited the other to watch television at his house. As his friend sat in the living room, he went to another room, picked up a pistol, came back in and shot him. He took a picture to show his gang what he had done. That was the price of loyalty. The incident shook the whole community of faith, and it set the stage for a change of direction for Tom Wilson.

He wanted to do something to help these kids stay out of gangs and find meaning in their lives, and God led him to launch a charter school under the auspices of the state, not the church. That's when he asked Scott to join him as co-pastor.

During those years, the church grew to about nine hundred three different times, but each time, it lost momentum and dropped back to about six hundred people. Scott went to a conference, and he realized that his vehicle simply wasn't capable of taking him to the destination of his vision. In his book *Steering Through Chaos*, he explains, "Instantly, I realized that the way we hired staff, designed our programs, and trained leaders worked really well up to about 900 people, but if we continued to follow our present methods, we'd keep hitting the same ceiling again and again. Change, I was convinced, was absolutely necessary, but as I sat in that conference room..., my vision for the future was tempered by the stunning reality that change required hard decisions that would create tremendous pain for me, my family, our staff, and the lay leaders of our church."[1]

Scott and his father realized that they were serving in an antiquated organizational system with inherent role confusion between the two of them and between the church and the new charter school. They began to carefully but boldly destroy the old in order to build something new. Tom left the pastorate to devote his energies to establishing charter schools around the nation, and God is using him in incredible ways.[2] Scott became the senior pastor. God led him to begin a new church several miles south of Dallas in Red Oak, while keeping the previous campus as a satellite.

Over the past several years, Scott has worked hard to create a strong, healthy, inspiring culture for his board and his staff, and the results are amazing. They currently have five campuses in the Dallas area with several thousand in attendance. But that's just what people see on the surface. As we've noticed throughout this book, culture is what flows in the organizational bloodstream, not just what's skin deep.

I've been consulting with Scott for several years. He's a remarkable leader. He is always open to new ideas; in fact, he's a sponge. He's more than a problem solver. In every situation, he wants to dig deeper to uncover hidden truths. He seldom (if ever) jumps to conclusions. Instead, he asks questions, pursues insights, and involves people in the process all along the way. Then, when they come to a decision, he has the buy-in of his team and the confirmation that he is on the right track. As I've talked to Scott about the importance of culture, he immediately grasped the principles I've shared in this book, even before they were ever committed to paper or shared at events. People on his staff are convinced that he loves them and values their contribution to the vision of the church. His affirmations come from his heart, so people don't have to wonder if his praise is genuine. He has created a culture of experimentation in which he and his team challenge each other to attempt great things for God—without fear that failure will be condemned. They certainly strive for excellence, but they never neglect the spice of creativity in all they do. Scott's blend of vision, creativity, and authentic relationships lowers walls of resistance and builds trust with his staff, his board, people who attend the church, and those in the community. The culture of this church is so inspiring that people can't wait to get involved there!

> Scott has created a culture of experimentation in which he and his team challenge each other to attempt great things for God—without fear that failure will be condemned.

Some leaders put on a good face in public, but they aren't very good at capturing the hearts and winning the loyalty of those closest to them. That's not the case with Scott. He has learned to be a shrewd judge of character and skills. One of his best hires is Justin Lathrop, whose leadership style is the perfect complement to Scott's. Justin works tirelessly behind the scenes to put all the pieces in place in the grand design of the church's vision and strategy. These two men are both better leaders because they found each other, and they aren't threatened in the least by the other's consummate abilities.

Over time, Scott transformed the culture of the church board. Years ago, they were tasked, like most church boards, with handling mounds of minutia. Gradually, Scott gave them more authority to have input in the larger issues of vision and strategy. Board members now feel empowered and valued because they know they are part of the top leadership team of the church. Any turf wars from the past have been drowned in the tidal wave of caring about God's kingdom instead of the price of copy paper.

Scott is an outstanding leader because he is an excellent learner. When he began the process of change, he was as lost in the woods as anyone else. But he wasn't content to let things stay the way they had always been. He believed God wanted something better in his church's culture, and he was open to learning how to make the necessary changes. That's what it takes: a little insight, a little creativity, a little courage, and a lot of love.

A Question About Music Style

William is the pastor of a church in Tennessee. He heard me explain the importance of creating an inspiring culture on his team and in his church, and went home ready to take bold steps forward. He patiently explained to his leadership team the principles of capturing momentum at point A, and he helped them understand the necessity of changing the vehicle so that they could fulfill their vision. As the months went by, the team implemented new ways of relating to each other, valuing those who ask hard questions, and creating new feedback loops to be sure everyone was on board. They also began to craft a new vehicle. As always, some members of his team adopted the new concepts very early, but some needed a few more questions answered.

As they talked about changing the style of music, the pastor realized that the people in the congregation—and especially those who didn't yet know Christ—responded more positively to more contemporary songs. The praise and worship leaders, Joel and his wife, Liz, had been with the church for over eight years. The band, the choir, and the congregation loved them, but when William talked to them about changing music styles, they were adamant that they shouldn't change. During a month of weekly staff meetings, William shared his heart and his vision for the church, and he patiently explained how he believed the new worship style would have a powerful impact on people. But Joel dug in his heels. His intensity had been rising in each meeting, and now he leaned forward and glared at William. "If we change our style of music, I won't be true to my calling from God. I can't and I won't do that!"

Suddenly William realized that the issue for Joel (and, he assumed, for Liz too) was not about the preference for a particular music style, but about personal integrity. I'm not sure what Joel saw in William's face at that moment, but he must have thought he held all the cards. He growled at William, "And if you insist on changing direction with the music, then you're abandoning God's calling, and *you* have a problem with integrity!" Joel had raised the stakes, and he pushed all his chips to the center of the table. He called William's bet, but he lost. William calmly replied, "Joel, I'm sorry you feel that way. I don't see it as a matter of integrity. I just want to reach people with the love of Christ, and music is an important part in our efforts. I had hoped you would see the heart of this change and gladly be part of the team. If you can't, then it's best for you to leave."

> Joel had raised the stakes, and he pushed all his chips to the center of the table. He called William's bet, but he lost.

Joel stormed out in a huff. As it turns out, Liz had prompted Joel to frame their resistance as an integrity issue. They were both furious with William, and they felt betrayed by the rest of the leadership team because they supported him. As soon as the dust cleared, William met with Rich, the associate praise and worship leader, to find out where he stood. Rich had listened to both sides of the debate (which is what the discussion had become), but he came to a different conclusion. He told

William, "Pastor, I'd prefer the music style we've been using since I've been here, but if you believe God is leading us to touch more people just by changing our worship, I'm for it."

William was pleasantly surprised, and it must have shown on his face, because Rich continued, "Pastor, it's not really about the music. It's about the kingdom. I want to honor God and reach people. That's what I understand you want to do. God gave you a vision, and I'm here to serve. I'll be glad to help any way I can."

Rich became the praise and worship leader, and he's doing a great job in his new position. The new music style seems to be having a positive effect. It's hard to tell why more unbelievers and new believers are coming, but they say they love the music! William and his team experienced chaos when they took steps to change their culture. It's inevitable. He understood the risks, and he anticipated that people on his team would respond all along the Diffusion of Innovations bell curve. He had a good idea whom he could count on to be the early embracers, but he was surprised that Joel and Liz proved to be never embracers. He thought it might be Rich or someone else, but he was ready for every possible response.

Asking the Right Questions

To take a team through the labyrinth of changing the culture, we need to engage their hearts and minds. Gifted teachers know that asking a great question is often more valuable than an hour of brilliant lecture. Questions challenge a person's thinking and draw her into the process of exploring solutions. The best ones are open questions that don't have simple, quick answers. They ask why and how, not just what and who. Sometimes, though, a simple question (and its answer) provides the foundation for a richer, deeper, more thought-provoking open question that follows it.

> Gifted teachers know that asking a great question is often more valuable than an hour of brilliant lecture.

First, ask yourself poignant questions. I'd suggest the following:

Personal Reflection

- Who am I? Where does my identity come from?

- What matters most to me?

- How well does my daily schedule relate to what matters most to me?

- Beyond roles and paychecks, what is my deepest, most compelling motivation? Really?

- How do I define success?

- Where am I in the process of learning, growing, and changing as a person and as a leader?

Don't rush your answers. Carve out some time alone, away from the hectic pace of the office, so you can genuinely ponder these things. Ask God to give insight into your heart, your desires, and your values—and listen to His Spirit as you think and pray. Leaders report that some answers come easily, but when they are committed to being ruthlessly honest with God, some questions challenge them to the core. Don't feel that you have to have all the answers tied up with a nice bow. Give yourself room to keep thinking, praying, and reflecting on your deepest motivations.

In a series of conversations with your team, ask them some penetrating questions. Listen carefully to their answers without correcting them or defending your positions. You'll know you're really listening if, when someone says something you don't agree with, you reply, "That's a very interesting point. Tell me more." I suggest you ask these questions:

Questions About the Team's Perception of the Leader

- What are three things you'd like to change about our team?

- What are three things you want to be sure we don't change?

- What do you want me to do for you?

+ What are you afraid I'm going to do?

+ What helps you serve with a full heart? What hinders or clouds your motivation?

+ Is there anything lingering in your mind or on your heart that you want to talk about? Nothing is off-limits; anything goes.

These questions are open enough to encompass the full range of challenges, relationships, systems, and motivations on a team. In fact, if the conversation doesn't go deeper than the level of job descriptions, it hasn't touched people's hearts. I'd also recommend that you use the questions in each section of the CULTURE analysis in Chapter Three. There's no time limit or deadline for completing these conversations. The process of discovery and disclosure is at least as important as the topics your team discusses. Opening lines of communication to talk about the things people have longed to discuss builds trust for the future.

> Opening lines of communication to talk about the things people have longed to discuss builds trust for the future.

Many pastors and teams also invite input about the culture from a wider range of midlevel leaders. They may ask each ministry director to schedule times to involve her staff and top volunteers, or the pastor may want to hold a town hall meeting. Large meetings are expedient, but they aren't conducive to the kinds of interactions needed to talk openly about the culture of the ministry team. I'd recommend that the ministry leaders follow the example of the pastor and lead their teams in open dialogue about the things that matter to them. The following are some questions for these teams:

Questions About the Team's Planning and Process

+ How well do people on our team understand how our work fits into the overall vision of the church?

+ In what ways are we celebrating success and affirming people for their contributions?

+ Do people on the team and the volunteers under them feel empowered and appreciated? Why or why not?

+ In what ways does our operating system (delegation, meetings, reporting, follow up, and so on) provide a forum for honest dialogue among team members and the ministry leader? How does the system hinder this kind of dialogue?

+ Do we have the tools and resources we need to fulfill God's vision for our team? If not, what do we need?

+ How well do we cultivate a culture of experimentation that celebrates taking risks to accomplish great things for God?

+ How well are we identifying, selecting, and developing rising leaders in our pipeline?

Be aware that asking these questions (and others from the CULTURE analysis in Chapter Three) often surfaces perceptions that can be inflammatory. Leading a team through the chaos of culture change is challenging work, but don't let the left hand of dread and the right hand of fear squeeze hope from the hearts of your team. Invite open dialogue, but always communicate that you and the team will trust God together to find solutions. Leaders rise to meet challenges, and as Napoleon remarked, "Leaders are dealers in hope."

Don't let your team get stuck in the past. Invite team members to be honest in their assessment and creative in finding answers. In all these discussions, teams have four needs (much like a family that is going through a significant change). These are:

1. The need for clarity

2. The need for the leader to model steady emotions, avoiding extreme highs and lows

3. The need to take action after decisions are made and the new direction is set

4. The need for security in unsettling times

In holding all these important discussions, realize that leaders are abstract communicators, but most team members think more concretely. Abstract communicators can add concrete points and illustrations to make sure they connect with people, but the vast majority of concrete thinkers have difficulty internalizing abstract thoughts. Those concepts bore them; they want specifics. For example, the pastor shares his vision: "God wants us to reach this community with the Good News of Christ." As Sally listens with the rest of the team, she wonders, "When he says 'community,' does he mean the people who live in a one-mile radius of the church, or five miles out?" But that's not her only concrete question. She also wants to know, "What kind of training will they provide for us? I'll tell you, if they have the training on Thursday night, I can't come because I have to take my daughter to piano practice. And if Jim is leading the training, I'm not going to go whenever it's offered. I don't like him at all."

Sally's thinking process isn't wrong. It's just concrete. Pastors need to understand that the vast majority of people on their teams and in their churches don't separate vision from strategy, which includes specific plans, meetings, roles, and schedules. It's a mistake for abstract-thinking pastors to share their vision one week and their strategy the next. They'll lose people that way. When pastors realize that their people's minds are quickset concrete, they'll make sure to simultaneously share specific plans and details of their global vision.

The leader's example of honesty and faith sets the tone for the team's future. If everyone feels like an integral part, everyone will contribute her best. Honesty invites long-buried emotions to come to the surface, so conflict is inevitable. Don't be surprised, but don't let conflict cloud the team's future. Welcome honest dialogue and seek resolution for each issue. Keep pointing people to God, His provision for the future, and His purpose for the team and the church. The way your team learns to relate to each other sets the tone for the culture of the church.

Change with Grace

All change is a critique of the past. If we're not careful, we can step on the toes of those we're trying to lead as we destroy the old vehicle and create a new one. Leaders need to understand what's at stake in the hearts of those who treasure the past. They may not be thrilled to change vehicles! We can't improve anything without changing it. The conundrum of leadership is this: people want improvement, but they resist change. Our task is helping them learn to embrace change.

> The conundrum of leadership is this: people want improvement, but they resist change.

The vocabulary of change is very important. As we lead people to capture momentum at point A and change vehicles, we need to avoid labeling the current systems as "bad" or "ineffective," or using any other language that devalues the hard work and dedication of those who have come before us. To help people take steps into the future, we need to celebrate the past. When they feel that we truly value the past, they will be willing to let go of it and take steps forward.

When I was a pastor of a church in Michigan years ago, we realized that we needed to replace the old single-pane windows that were scant protection against the frigid winter winds. We raised enough money to have top-quality, triple-paned windows installed. When the man from the window company came to get measurements of our eight windows, he called me over and said, "Pastor, there's a problem. The windows aren't all the same size, and they aren't all a standard size. We're going to have to customize some of the windows. I'm afraid the price is going to be significantly higher. Do you want to proceed?"

I called a board member, Brother Bolen, to come to the church to talk about this problem. As we inspected the building more carefully and took precise measurements, we found that one wall was 18 inches longer than the other—an additional block had been added to that wall during construction many years before I arrived. As Brother Bolen and I took measurements, I began to complain about the shoddy construction of the church. "Why in the world," I said in disgust, "would anyone build a building this way? Didn't they know better?"

Brother Bolen shuffled his feet and said in a quiet voice, "Brother Sam, we did the best we could in those days." He paused, then continued. "We worked in the oil fields during the day, and we came to the church at night to build it. This area was a swamp, but we filled it in with wheelbarrow loads of dirt trucked in. The light wasn't very good, and some of us had never built anything before. I'm sorry. We did the best we could."

I hoped that Jesus would come back in that instant or, better yet, that the earth would open and swallow me so I'd never have to see Brother Bolen again. I had hurt the feelings of a man I loved. I had focused only on the change necessary for the future without a thought about the values and commitment of men and women in the past.

I learned a valuable lesson that day. Sometime later, I wanted to change the paneling in the church. It was the best they could afford when the church was built, but it was ugly—incredibly ugly. This time, though, I realized that I needed to honor the past in order to change it. I preached a four-message series called "If the Walls Could Talk." I interviewed people who had been at the church for many years, and I told their stories: this person was saved here, that couple got married, this student was baptized, and God changed that family forever. To prepare for the third Sunday, I asked people to bring their old family Bibles that contained their spiritual histories, and I asked them to bring markers so they could write on the walls. That Sunday, they shared pictures of loved ones, told stories and cried happy tears, and asked for prayer for people who were still lost without Christ. They wrote cherished names and personal notes on the paneling during that service, and we poured out our hearts to celebrate all God had done within those walls. They knew that the next day, the workmen were coming to put sheetrock over the old paneling and paint it a beautiful color. They weren't going to rip it out and replace it. As a testimony of the past, we left the paneling and the names written on it for as long as that building would stand.

In their minds (or maybe on paper), leaders need to keep a ledger during times of change. On one side of the ledger are gains, and on the other, losses. The leader casting the vision for change can list many things under gains. She sees the future, and she is convinced that the changes she proposes will propel the church to fulfill God's vision. A few other visionaries are in that column, too, but virtually everyone else, about 95 percent of the people, feels a genuine sense of loss because of the proposed change. Even small changes to a church threaten people's stability and their sense of history. Someone might grumble, "I don't want to meet in the new building because my husband and I were married in our worship center. It means the world to me." Losses always carry emotional weight.

As we stand in the pulpit or meeting room to extol the wonderful benefits of the change we are inaugurating, we feel excited about the glorious possibilities, but the vast majority of people listening to us feel only sadness. No wonder they are resistant. If we don't connect with their hearts and win them, they start to question our motives and our wisdom to lead them. To bring them along, we have to recognize their losses, celebrate the past, grieve with them, and lead them gently into the future. If we don't take these compassionate steps, we effectively communicate that we don't care about their feelings or their history. In our

> All change is a critique of the past, and we need to be sensitive and wise as we talk about the past our people treasure.

communication about change, we want them to be convinced, "He understands what's meaningful to me. He wants to move us forward, but he celebrates the past. I can follow a leader like that."

My walk with Brother Bolen that day at the church gave me valuable insight about change. It was a hard lesson, but one I'll never forget. All change is a critique of the past, and we need to be sensitive and wise as we talk about the past our people treasure. We simply can't take them forward unless they are convinced that we treasure their past, too.

Quo Vadis

Now, at the end of the book, which way will you go? This is not the kind of book that you breeze through, picking up a principle or two and moving on to something else. Either you embrace the process of transforming a culture and devote yourself to the hard but rewarding work, or you put the book down and go back to business as usual. There's not much middle ground. Those who take up the challenge are in for the ride of their lives. Very few tasks are as stimulating and difficult, but seeing a culture change in front of our eyes is a glorious thing to behold. The early stage is often the most difficult. Misunderstandings and resistance threaten to stop us in our tracks, but if we have the courage to keep moving forward, people begin to get it, and they become allies. Changing the culture of a team or a church forces us to delve below the surface and confront our motives and our systems. It's not for the fainthearted, but it's worth it. I hope you're in—all in.

Think About It . . .

1. How might the questions listed in this chapter help you and your team begin the process of changing your culture?

2. How have you seen leaders implement change with grace? Why is it crucial to identify with people's losses about the past as you help them take steps into the future?

3. What's the next step for you? How will you take it? What do you expect in the next month as you take that step with your team?

APPENDIX 1

OVERVIEW OF THE
FREE CULTURE SURVEY

www.samchandculturesurvey.com

This survey was developed by Dr. Samuel R. Chand, Mr. Pat Springle, Professor Tom Snider, and Mrs. Melinda R. Keeney to help senior leaders and their organizations obtain an accurate assessment of the culture of their organizations and teams. Each factor of the team's life and health will be graded and reported as:

Inspiring...Accepting...Stagnant...
Discouraging...Toxic

The survey measures individual perceptions of the **seven** key components of **CULTURE**: Control, Understanding, Leadership, Trust, Unafraid, Responsive, and Execution.

This survey can be used by teams as small as three members or as large as two hundred.

To complete the survey, go to http://www.samchandculturesurvey. com and sign up the senior leader and the team. Enter the name and e-mail address of each person on the team to be surveyed. An e-mail will be sent to team members to invite him or her   to come to the site and fill out the survey. If team members haven't come to the site in a reasonable period of time, they'll receive an e-mail to remind them.

When all surveys have been completed, an e-mail will be sent to the senior leader notifying him or her that the results are available for viewing. The report will include a rating of the team on each of the seven CULTURE components, along with a written summary of the results and suggestions for enhancing the team culture.

To build a more positive, productive culture, teams may benefit from reading and discussing this book.

www.samchandculturesurvey.com

APPENDIX 2

STRATEGIC PLANNING GRID

What	Why	Who	How	When	Where	How Much	Accountable to Whom	Evaluation Process

© Dr. Samuel R. Chand

APPENDIX 3

TO-DO LIST AND STATUS REPORT FOR *MAJOR* ITEMS

Department:

Responsible Person:

Date:

	Item	Date Item Received	Status	Projected Completion Ddate	Actual Completion Date
1.					
2.					
3.					
4.					

All people making reports should do the following four things:

1. Report *data*.

2. Create meaning by providing *implications* of the data.

3. *Recommend* actions for the implications.

4. Be ready with *strategies* once recommendation(s) have been confirmed.

© Dr. Samuel R. Chand

APPENDIX 4

SURVEY – OVERALL SURVEY RESULT TEMPLATE

About the free Culture Survey:

When you and your organization choose to take the Culture Survey at samchandculturesurvey.com, you will receive, free of charge, results that measure your organization's culture with empirical data, as well as an explanation on why your organization received that score and what to do about it.

			Before filtering		After filtering
Partial responses (unique respondents)					
Completed responses (unique respondents)					
Score	Mean	Std dev	25% quartile	Median	75% quartile
Total score					
Control					
Understanding					
Leadership					
Trust					
Unafraid					
Responsive					
Execution					

Leader:

The number of your team members who have taken the survey will be shown in the area marked: Completed Responses>After Filtering.

Once this box matches your number of participating team members, your score is final.

Your score will change and not be valid until ALL participants have completed the survey. Only then will the **'Mean'** column reflect your true and final score.

The actual translation of the numbers are as follows:

10 thru 18.4 = Toxic

18.5 thru 26.4 = Discouraging

26.5 thru 34.4 = Stagnant

34.5 thru 42.4 = Accepting

42.5 thru 50 = Inspiring

Score Possibilities for: Control

Inspiring

Your team is a model of clear lines of authority and delegated responsibility. Team members regularly ask clarifying questions to be sure information is flowing smoothly and resources are readily available. Bottlenecks may occur, but they are identified and resolved fairly quickly. The system provides excellent feedback, affirmation and course correction. In fact, leaders give plenty of attention to clarifying authority, facilitating coordination, and providing resources for team members.

Accepting

People on your team generally know who is responsible for delegated tasks. When bottlenecks occur, people on the team often, but not always, identify and resolve them. A few people on the team are slow to give feedback and provide collaborative support. Leaders can give more attention to creating a more effective system of collaboration and feedback.

Stagnant

Your team experiences significant bottlenecks from time to time, and a few of them may have become chronic problems. It only takes one person to create a systemic and troublesome bottleneck. If it isn't addressed, it can erode the energy of a team. On this team, there isn't a regular arena or time to clarify lines of authority so people make a lot of assumptions about who is responsible and how tasks will be done. Problems with authority and delegated responsibility aren't addressed until someone "has had it!"

Discouraging

On this team, power and control may in the hands of only one or two people, or perhaps the team experiences the opposite problem: nobody knows who's responsible for anything. Either way, people on the team feel discouraged and isolated. They aren't challenged to do their best because they don't know what's expected of them, and they don't feel appreciated when they try hard. A person who isn't the leader may be the power broker in this environment.

Toxic

Your team experiences confusion and resentment because people don't know what's expected of them. One person may be the ultimate power broker and insist on controlling every person's activities, or perhaps no one knows what's going on, so everyone feels out of control. On teams like this, collaboration is virtually nonexistent, and each person is angry and defensive. Bottlenecks have become such a way of life that nobody even notices the frustration and inefficiency they cause.

Score Possibilities for: Understanding

Inspiring

People on your team can clearly articulate the vision and goals of the team, and they can explain each person's specific role. The leader invites people to ask any question at any time, and he values open dialogue. When conflicts arise, they are addressed quickly and thoroughly. The leader invests significant time and resources in team building: understanding, listening, supporting, encouraging, and celebrating each other's successes.

Accepting

Most of the people on the team have a good understanding of the overall vision of the team, their specific roles, and the contributions of others on the team. A few people, however, may not have a clear picture of vision, goals, and individual roles. There may be a few simmering conflicts that haven't been resolved. On some occasions, these unresolved problems make people somewhat defensive instead of giving whole-hearted support to one another.

Stagnant

A few people on the team may have a clear grasp of their roles, but they often act in isolation. Staff meetings are often cover the list of tasks to delegate, with little if any genuine give and take. People on the team are like billiard balls bouncing off each other, except for a few close cliques of people who get together to complain about the leadership.

Discouraging

People on the team aren't really sure how to connect the overall vision of the organization with their specific roles, and even more, they don't collaborate to maximize the team's potential. People on the team have little appreciation for each other, and they don't even understand how they might work together more effectively. Tension is a normal part of team relationships because conflict isn't adequately addressed.

Toxic

People on this team are either fiercely (and blindly) loyal to their leader, apathetic because they feel their contributions don't count, or deeply resentful because they feel used. Without a clear, compelling, and shared vision, staff members are suspicious of the leader's motives. Conspiracies form as people seek solace from other disgruntled team members.

Score Possibilities for: Leadership

Inspiring

The organization's strategy of leadership development is clearly defined and effectively implemented. It includes identifying rising leaders, then selecting, equipping, placing, and overseeing them. The team leader invests considerable resources in leadership development. In fact, it's one of the chief values of the organization.

Accepting

On this team, the strategy of developing leaders may be clear, but the implementation needs some attention. Or perhaps, the strategy may not be as clear and comprehensive as it needs to be, but people see a lot of value in developing leaders. The organization is seeing a significant pool of people rising into positions of leadership, but some are slipping through the cracks due to inattention.

Stagnant

A few team members are doing a good job of investing in leadership development, but there isn't an effective overall strategy for the team. Team leaders may talk a good game, but the implementation is lacking in some way. They may be focusing on training people in skills instead of developing character and heart in rising leaders. Instead of pursing people with leadership potential, existing leaders assume, "If other people want to be leaders, they'll ask to be developed."

Discouraging

In this organization, there is a chronic shortage of competent leaders. The existing leaders haven't invested attention and resources in identifying, selecting, equipping, and placing rising leaders, and frankly, they don't see it as a priority. They are trying to protect their own positions instead of developing others as leaders. The result is that the staff and key volunteers feel burdened by unrealistic demands. They are overworked and underappreciated.

Toxic

In toxic organizations, the top leader demands allegiance, and he sees leadership development as a threat to his position. He may say he's committed to developing leaders, but he only wants people who are "yes men" and "yes women." He seldom celebrates when others succeed. People feel used and resentful, but they may be afraid to leave because those who look elsewhere are branded as "disloyal."

Score Possibilities for: Trust

Inspiring

To build a team with a high level of trust, leaders carefully select team members who have high integrity and the skills to resolve inevitable conflict that arises, even on the best teams, from time to time. Leaders invest time and attention in building trust because they know that it is both essential and fragile. The team has clear policies and practices about gossip, confidentiality, and conflict resolution.

Accepting

Generally, the team is characterized by relationships that are honest, open, and transparent. There may be a few unresolved conflicts that erode the team's level of trust. Sooner or later, the leader (or someone else) picks up on these and addresses them. In most cases, people see failure as a stepping stone for future success, not a tragedy to be blamed on the one who failed.

Stagnant

This team lives with significant unresolved tension. The attitude of most people on the team, though, is, "Don't worry about it. That's just the way life is here." Team members see each other as trustworthy or untrustworthy, or more specifically, as good people and bad people. They form alliances, and they gossip about people who aren't in their clique.

Discouraging

On this team, there have been serious breaches of trust, but these haven't been adequately addressed and resolved. The simmering suspicion clouds relationships and seriously affects the team's effectiveness. People form alliances for self-protection. Failure is blasted by those who distrust the responsible person, but the person who failed is fiercely defended by those in his alliance. People spend more time analyzing each other, taking sides, and gossiping than working together to fulfill God's vision.

Toxic

Distrust is a way of life for people on this team. People see incongruence in leadership, and they feel isolated and angry. Conflict is constant and brutal, and alliances form for self-preservation. The leaders focus only on production, not on building the team. Any hint of disloyalty is dealt with harshly, so people feel very insecure.

Score Possibilities for: Unafraid

Inspiring

Leaders on this team model courage in the face of opportunities, difficulties, heartaches, and losses. They face the risks of innovation and all forms of trouble with a powerful blend of honesty and hope. Facing challenges with true faith is a clear value of the team. They don't engage in mindless "happy talk"; instead, they seek God's wisdom and support from one another as they face challenges. They celebrate courage when they see it in each other and people throughout the organization.

Accepting

This team values innovation and moves ahead with enthusiasm. It also honestly faces difficulties with a sense of optimism. Sometimes, expressions of courage border on "happy talk," but most of the time, people wed wisdom with bold faith. A few people on the team are a bit slow to come around. Their sour dispositions threaten to cloud the team's bold sense of optimism as they tackle difficult issues.

Stagnant

The team has a few brave souls who launch out to attempt great things, but fearful people on the team question their motives. Instead of valuing innovation, too many people are more interested in eliminating risks to avoid any chance of failure. To be sure they can't fail, they ask a thousand questions and engage in endless delays. They want to guarantee success, so they miss many opportunities.

Discouraging

People on this team avoid risks as a way of life because they are afraid of being blamed when anything goes wrong. To them, failure is a catastrophe. They also fail to handle life's troubles and losses with a strong sense of faith. They complain and feel like victims of life's circumstances. To move forward, they have to have all their questions answered, and even then, they may not take a single step. Because they live in fear, they seldom take advantage of any opportunity.

Toxic

In this punitive environment, any failure is harshly condemned, so team members spend their time building walls to protect themselves.

They avoid any risks, hiding behind a deluge of memos, charts, and the need "to do more research." When someone on the team experiences a problem, a few come to console, but most team members avoid the person because they don't want to take the risk to get involved.

Score Possibilities for: Responsive

Inspiring

The team leader and members are perceptive about opportunities and threats they face. They regularly ask each other for input and advice, and they welcome outside input that can help them respond to situations more effectively. They are always learning and trying new methods to gain insight and skills. Leaders value the whole team's participation, so they invest time and energy to get buy-in from everyone on the team. Details are important to this team, and very few things fall through the cracks.

Accepting

Team members invest time and energy to communicate and collaborate between departments. They value each other's input and seek excellence in serving people. They may let a few things fall through the cracks, but when they become aware of these things, they make adjustments. Generally, they value outside input to help them be more effective, but they may not seek it often enough.

Stagnant

Some members of the team are conscientious and responsive to meet other's needs, but pockets of lethargy rob the team of enthusiasm and excellence. Perhaps some of the people aren't clear about their responsibility and roles. The team leader makes a lot of assumptions about how things "ought to go," but doesn't create and manage systems that regularly analyze opportunities and threats. They may do an analysis of an event, but they seldom do anything different next time.

Discouraging

Staff members see each other as competitors rather than collaborators, so silos are the norm for the organization. People are more interested in defending their own turf than fulfilling the vision of the organization and helping each other be successful. Without attention to detail, many things fall through the cracks, and the team receives lots of complaints from those they are supposed to serve.

Toxic

Departmental isolation, known as "silos," are a way of life for this team. People spend their time and energies defending their own positions instead of collaborating to provide solutions. Team members are defensive and fiercely competitive. They feel threatened by outside input, so they become intellectually lethargic and emotionally numb. People on the outside wonder why the team doesn't give them time and attention.

Score Possibilities for: Execution

Inspiring

The team has crystal clear goals, lines of authority, and schedules. People understand their roles, and they work hard to fulfill their assignments according to the deadlines. The leaders provide adequate resources for every task. To make sure projects are completed with excellence and on time, the team has an effective feedback loop. And they regularly celebrate every success.

Accepting

The team has an effective system in place to clarify goals and individual's roles. Most of the time, people work well together to meet deadlines and work effectively, but a few who fail to do their part occasionally slow the team. The leader addresses this problem from time to time, but it doesn't seem to change.

Stagnant

The team gets some things done fairly well, but they lack the fire and drive to be a truly effective team. No matter what the project is, something always seems to be missing: clear goals, identified roles of each team member, resources, feedback and communication, or something else. Every time failure occurs, people are quick to point at someone else to blame.

Discouraging

Too often when the team tackles a task, several pieces of the puzzle are missing: clear goals, identified roles of each team member, collaboration, resources, feedback, or deadlines met. Consistent failure and lack of accountability ruins the atmosphere of the team. People lose enthusiasm for their work, and they constantly blame others for their problems.

Toxic

Leaders may rant and rave that they won't accept failure any longer, but nothing changes, or they may have given up entirely on the team having any impact. Chronic failure can be traced to a number of problems, including poor modeling by the top leaders and a systemic breakdown of roles, goals, resources, and deadlines. Doing a poor job has become normalized, so attempts by individual staff members to do an excellent job are considered a threat to the rest of the team. Lethargy, then, is rewarded and institutionalized.

NOTES

Chapter 1: Culture Trumps Vision

1. Dick Clark quoted in "Corporate Culture Is the Game," *Executive Leadership*, Nov. 2008, p. 3.

2. Patrick Lencioni, *The Five Dysfunctions of a Team* (San Francisco: Jossey-Bass, 2002), pp. 188–189.

3. Archibald Hart, *The Crazy-Making Workplace* (Ann Arbor, Mich.: Vine Books, 1993), p. 67.

4. Chuck Colson and Jack Eckerd, *Why America Doesn't Work* (New York: Random House, 1994).

Chapter 3: Seven Keys of Culture

1. Note: Most assessment tools used in organizations measure an individual's temperament or aptitude. Teams can use some of the best tools to show how each person tends to respond to others. The free CULTURE survey is available online. To sign up for your team, go to www.samchandculturesurvey.com.

2. Samuel R. Chand, *Who's Holding Your Ladder?* (Niles, Ill.: Mall Publishing, 2003), p. 62.

3. Shayla McKnight, "Workplace Gossip? Keep It to Yourself," *New York Times*, Nov. 14, 2009, http://www.nytimes.com/2009/11/15/jobs/15pre.html?_r=2.

4. "Spirit Lexicon," *Spirit*, Dec. 2009, p. 56.

5. "Bain & Company" (interview with Steve Ellis), *Consulting*, Sept.-Oct. 2008, p. 19.

6. Keith Sawyer quoted in Janet Rae-Dupree, "Teamwork, the True Mother of Invention," *New York Times*, Dec. 7, 2008, p. B3.

Chapter 4: Vocabulary Defines Culture

1. Joseph Mattera, "Why a Church's Culture Always Trumps Its Vision," 2007, http://josephmattera.org/index.php?option=com_content&task=view&id=474&Itemid=1.

2. Maren and Jamie Showkeir, "How to Talk Straight in Hard Times," *Leader to Leader*, Summer 2009, p. 15.

3. Stone offers this definition in the Q&A section of her Web site, http://lindastone.net/qa.

Chapter 6: The Catalyst of Chaos

1. Adapted from Julia Kirby and Thomas A. Stewart, "The Institutional Yes," *Harvard Business Review*, Oct. 2007.

2. "Developing a Change-Friendly Culture" (interview with John P. Kotter), *Leader to Leader*, Spring 2008, pp. 33–38.

3. William L. White, *The Incestuous Workplace* (Center City, Minn.: Hazeldon, 1997), p. 51.

4. "Developing a Change-Friendly Culture," p. 36.

5. Adapted from "Drop the Ax on Mediocrity," *Executive Leadership*, May 2008, 23(5), 1.

6. "The Really New Waldorf" (interview with Eric O. Long), *Leaders*, Jan. 2004, 27, 80.

7. Linda Hudson quoted in "Fitting In, and Rising to the Top," *New York Times*, Sept. 20, 2009, http://www.nytimes.com/2009/09/20/business/20corner.html.

Chapter 7: Changing Vehicles

1. Henry Moore quoted in John A. Byrne, "Celebrating the Ordinary," *Fast Company*, Jan. 2005, p. 14.

2. Jim Baker, "Achieve Peak Performance with a Leadership Culture of Shared Purpose," *Church Executive*, July 2008, pp. 76–78.

3. Dave Logan, John King, and Halee Fisher-Wright, "Corporate Tribes: The Heart of Effective Leadership," *Leader to Leader*, Summer 2008, pp. 25–29.

Chapter 8: Yes, You Can!

1. Scott Wilson, *Steering Through Chaos* (Grand Rapids, Mich.: Zondervan, 2009).

2. To find out more about Dr. Wilson, charter schools, and consulting to help communities launch effective charter schools, go to www.nationalcharterconsultants.com.

ABOUT THE AUTHOR

Dr. Samuel R. Chand, having been raised in a pastor's home in India, is uniquely equipped to share his passion to mentor, develop, and inspire leaders in ministry and the marketplace. Dr. Chand has served as senior pastor, college president, chancellor, and president emeritus of Beulah Heights University, the country's largest predominantly African American Bible College.

Dr. Chand speaks regularly at leadership conferences, churches, corporations, ministerial conferences, seminars, and other leadership development opportunities. He was named one of the top thirty global leadership gurus by www.leadershipgurus.net. Dr. Chand serves on the board of EQUIP (Dr. John Maxwell's ministry), working with five million leaders worldwide, and assists Bishop Eddie L. Long's leadership development team. Dr. Chand works with leaders through leadership consultations and resources, including books and CDs, online mentoring, and speaking. Some of the books he has written are *Who's Holding Your Ladder?*, *LadderShifts*, and *Planning Your Succession*.

His educational background includes an honorary doctor of divinity degree from Heritage Bible College, a master of arts in biblical counseling from Grace Theological Seminary, and a bachelor of arts in biblical education from Beulah Heights University. Dr. Chand and his wife, Brenda, live in McDonough, Georgia, with their two daughters, Rachel and Deborah, and granddaughter, Adeline. You can learn more about Dr. Chand's ministry by visiting www.samchand.com.

OTHER BOOKS BY
DR. SAMUEL R. CHAND

Failure: The Womb of Success

Futuring: Leading Your Church into Tomorrow

Who's Holding Your Ladder? Selecting Your Leaders—Your Most Crucial Decision

Who Moved Your Ladder? Your Next Bold Move

What's Shakin' Your Ladder? 15 Challenges All Leaders Face

LadderShifts: New Realities—Rapid Change—Your Destiny

Ladder Focus: Creating, Sustaining, and Enlarging Your Big Picture

Planning Your Succession: Preparing for Your Future

ReChurch: When Change Is No Longer an Option

Master Leaders—a Collaborative Book with George Barna

Weathering the Storm: Leading in Uncertain Times

Leadership Pain: The Classroom for Growth

Bigger, Faster Leadership: Lessons from the Builders of the Panama Canal

www.samchand.com

THE SERVICES OF
DR. SAMUEL R. CHAND CONSULTING

Dr. Chand has only one product—LEADERSHIP. However, he delivers the product through three distinct systems:

1. Consultations: Every consultation is totally customized with four distinct components—Assess—Articulate—Align—Advance—leading to culture formation, vision fulfillment, capacity enhancement, and leadership development.

2. Speaking at leadership conferences and training events. Dr. Chand's busy speaking schedule covers a broad spectrum of churches, corporations, nonprofits, and other organizations.

3. Resources—books, CDs, DVDs, and online resources. Dr. Chand's resources continue to be used as reference guides by leaders globally. Among his many books, *Who's Holding Your Ladder?*, *LadderShifts*, *ReChurch*, and *Futuring* continue to engage and challenge leaders at all levels.

www.samchand.com